T0154481

Ten
Things
About
Writing

Joanne Harris MBE was born in Barnsley in 1964, of a French mother and an English father. She studied Modern and Mediaeval Languages at Cambridge and was a teacher for fifteen years, during which time she published three novels, including *Chocolat* (1999), which was made into an Oscar-nominated film starring Juliette Binoche.

Since then, she has written fifteen more novels, three novellas, including *Orfeia* (2020), two collections of short stories, a Doctor Who novella, guest episodes for the game Zombies Run, the libretti for two short operas, several screenplays, a musical and three cookbooks. Her books are now published in over fifty countries and have won a number of British and international awards. She is an honorary Fellow of St Catharine's College, Cambridge, has honorary doctorates in literature from the universities of Sheffield and Huddersfield.

She is a passionate advocate for authors' rights, and is currently the Chair of the Society of Authors and member of the Board of the Authors' Licensing and Collecting Society.

She works from a shed in her garden, plays bass in the band she first joined when she was sixteen and lives with her husband in a little wood in Yorkshire. You can find her on Twitter @joannechocolat.

Ten Things About Writing

JOANNE HARRIS

1 3 5 7 9 10 8 6 4 2

First published in 2020 by September Publishing

Copyright © Frogspawn Ltd 2020

Illustration copyright © Moose Allain 2020

The right of Joanne Harris to be identified as the author of this work
has been asserted by her in accordance with the Copyright Designs
and Patents Act 1988.

Typeset by Ed Pickford

Hardback ISBN 978-1-912836-59-8
Kindle ISBN 978-1-912836-64-2
Epub ISBN 978-1-912836-61-1

September Publishing
www.septemberpublishing.org

Contents

Introduction

Creative writing is a great deal more than just a professional skill. Yes, a good, clear, graphic style and the ability to tell a story can help in all kinds of professions, from teaching to advertising, from writing a marketing report to writing a bestselling novel; but making art for pleasure is a valid objective in itself. Writing for pleasure promotes articulacy, empathy, understanding, lateral thinking. It gives us insights into other lives; windows into other worlds. It allows us to harness our creative energy and gives us a sense of achievement. It's cheaper than therapy. Also it's *fun*. Fun is a worthwhile end in itself. And we tend to enjoy what we do well, and want to improve and build on our skills. I hope that this book will give you the chance to do just that, however far you choose to take it: whether you're a complete beginner, or an experienced writer looking to take your writing to the next level.

Part of improving your writing is learning what other writers have to say, and taking from them what is useful to you, which may vary from person to person. There is no single way to write, no cast-iron rules for making art, and what works for me may not work for you at all. That doesn't make either of us wrong. We all approach these things in our own ways – and, whatever your chosen method, if the end result satisfies you, if it gets the results you were hoping for, then you chose the right way for you. But here are some things that I have learnt over my years as a writer – I have shared some of them as part of a regular Twitter hashtag series, which some of you have found useful. Many of you have asked me to collect them and put them together into a book. So here they are: and whether your aim is to become a published writer or just to improve your written style, I hope you find something here to help, encourage or motivate you. Take what you need from these pages; and most of all, *enjoy what you do*. Joy is such a vital part of creative writing – because if you don't enjoy what you write, how can you expect anyone else to?

PART 1

Where Do I Start?

———

First novels ideally should be between
80,000 - 100,000 words.
I know about 2,000 words, so that's
about 50 times each. Easy!

1

Starting Out

There. That was easy, wasn't it? You've taken the first step already. You've decided to explore and expand your potential as a writer. Whatever your objective, it's a great thing to do, and I hope it will bring you joy and success in whatever you hope to achieve.

Now to look at a few ways to get you started.

1. Don't try to do too much at once. Although it may be true that a journey of a thousand miles begins with a single step, try not to think about where the journey will take you. Instead, try to focus on what you can do on a day-to-day basis.

2. Decide what you *want* from your writing. Do you write purely for your own pleasure? Do you write as therapy? Do you enjoy sharing your fan fiction online? Are you writing a story to entertain your grandchildren? Are you seeking to be published commercially? Whatever your reasons, and on whatever level you choose, writing can be a rewarding, enriching occupation that can bring joy to you and to others.

3. Manage your expectations. Don't assume that by writing you're going to make millions, attract girls (or boys), or get to hang out with famous people. For the most part, the best that will happen is that you'll do a lot of writing. Make sure that's what you *really* want. If you don't actually *enjoy* writing, you're unlikely to sustain the effort.

4. Manage your time. If you don't actively *make* time to write, then you'll never get round to it. (More on ways to do this in the next chapter.)

5. Manage your workspace. A designated workspace is the key to good writing habits. Decide where you are going to write and try to make it as accessible and as welcoming as possible. (More on your workspace later.)

6. Make sure you have the right tools to allow your writing to fit into your lifestyle. If you're on the move throughout the day, you might prefer a laptop or a writing app that you can use on your phone. If you're going to be working from home, you might prefer to work on a PC. And of course there's always the time-honoured notebook-and-pen combo . . .

7. Find a beta reader. Not everyone wants to share their work, but writing can be a lonely business. It can help to get feedback from a sympathetic, honest reader – and having an audience, even of one, can help with motivation.

8. Join an online community. It's so easy nowadays to get in touch with other writers, bloggers, editors or agents – and you can learn a lot from interacting with other people who may be on the same path.

9. Join the Society of Authors, or the Writers' Guild. (If you haven't been published yet, you can still join the society as an Associate Member or Friend). With its quarterly magazine, free legal advice, contract services, social events, literary prizes, grants and lectures on different aspects of publishing, it's well worth the membership fee.

10. Finally, *give yourself permission to write.* You can do it. It's allowed. No one's going to laugh at you or say you're not a proper writer – not anyone who matters, anyway.

Got it? Good.

Take a deep breath. You're on your way. Good luck, and may your writing bring you as much joy as mine has brought me . . .

2

Permission

A task that many new writers find unexpectedly difficult *is giving themselves permission to write.* They waste time and energy worrying: *Am I a proper writer? Will proper writers laugh at me? Am I being ridiculous in believing that actual readers might enjoy reading what I've written?* So here's a little checklist to help you get through this. And if you ever start to feel uncertain of yourself, come back to this page, take a deep breath, reread the list . . . then make yourself a cup of tea and get to work. You're allowed to do it. I said so.

1. Stop thinking in terms of 'proper' writers and the rest of the world. You're not an 'aspiring' writer, or an 'emerging' writer, or a 'budding' writer. If you write, you're a writer. So *write*!

2. Banish your fear of inadequacy. Do you write as well as you want to? Probably not. No writer does. But then, why would you be any different from any of the rest of us? We all have insecurities. We're all trying to improve our game. And like all games, yours will improve with practice, and with time.

3. Banish your writer's guilt. Ever feel guilty at the amount of time you spend watching TV, or reading, or exercising, or being with your friends? No? Then don't feel guilty at the time you spend writing. It's not a selfish indulgence, it's something you care about, and into which you're prepared to put work and energy. Make sure the people around you understand that, and support you. If they don't, find better people.

4. Stop comparing yourself to other writers. Compare your work to the last thing you wrote. If you're improving (and you *are*), you're doing fine.

5. Don't waste your time obsessing over getting an agent, or getting published, or thinking about all the money you think you'll make, or identifying market trends. Write until you have something worthwhile, then find someone to show it to. Anything else is just a distraction.

6. Find a support network. Online or off, it's comforting to know that there are others who feel as you do. Writing circles, blogger groups, fanfic communities, social media groups – all of these can help a writer feel connected. You are not alone, and the support of others can be an extraordinary comfort, especially if you hit a rough patch (and you will).

7. Establish a regular writing routine. Getting into the habit of writing is just like getting into any other habit – it takes a few weeks to establish. But stick with it; and before long it will feel as natural as any other part of your life.

8. Don't put yourself under unnecessary pressure. It can take a long time to get a book into publishable shape, so be careful how much you reveal to the people around you – that is, unless you want your colleagues at work constantly asking: 'How's the book going?'

9. Don't expect too much, too fast. Everything about writing a book takes a lot longer than you think it will. Live in hope, but pack for the long haul.

10. Don't worry if you end up trashing some or all of what you've written – nothing you write is ever wasted. Remember that every word you write is part of your ongoing training, and that anything you discard now may one day be reused, re-imagined or rebooted. For now, don't look back. You have work to do.

3

Habits

No one is born good at writing. The ability to spin words into gold is a skill that comes from hard work, patience and lots of practice. Some people may have an aptitude; others will struggle to gain momentum. And yet, whatever our writing ambitions – whether it's to create a bestseller, to self-publish a memoir, to write better fanfic or just to improve our blogging style – all of us can benefit from improving our writing skills.

Of course, we all have different styles and different approaches to writing; but getting into good habits can really make a difference. These are the ones I think are essential.

1. Read as much as you can. To be a writer, you *must* be a reader. Comics, games, fan fiction, literary fiction, commercial fiction, children's books, e-books, magazines, non-fiction – it's all part of your training. *All* reading is worthwhile. All reading teaches you something. Anyone telling you otherwise doesn't understand the nature of reading at all.

2. Read outside your comfort zone. We all have our favourite writers, and we often write in similar genres. To avoid going stale, occasionally swap your usual genre for something different: fiction for popular science; crime fiction for fantasy; fiction for non-fiction. Read widely: newspapers, comics, bestsellers, biographies, genre fiction. Nothing – *nothing* – you read is ever wasted.

3. Look off the page. Writing isn't limited to blogs and books. It's part of almost every aspect of our lives. You can learn a lot about fiction from a well-written film, a stage play, TV show, a game. Be aware of the quality of the writing you encounter. Be critical. Learn to identify what works and what doesn't, and why.

4. Get into the groove. However much or how little time you have, try to write *something* every day. Even if it's only a sentence, it helps you stay in the world you're creating. And once you're in that world, your mind will be quietly working on your plot and characters throughout the day.

5. Don't forget to daydream. Most writing happens *away* from your desk. So make room for some thinking time – whether that's a morning walk, a run, an hour's commute, or a long, relaxing bath. Switch off your phone whenever you can. These are often the times when inspiration strikes. Learn to identify it when it does.

6. Be observant. The best writers seem to *notice* more than the average person does – and then they show what they've seen to the reader. So watch the people around you; notice their mannerisms and behaviour. Watch the clouds; recall your dreams; remember colours, tastes and scents. You'll soon find you're noticing many more things – and they'll all help improve your writing.

7. Keep a notebook. Carry it with you at all times. In it, record anything you see or hear that you find interesting, new, striking, shocking, funny, singular. Dreams and day-dreams; thoughts and ideas. You never know what might fit into a story one day.

8. Read aloud. Words are like music; they have their own rhythms and beats. Reading aloud helps you understand the ebb and flow of the language.

9. Don't write because you want to be a writer. Write because *you want to write*. If you don't actively enjoy what you're doing, you'll never have the staying power to finish even a first draft.

10. Don't beat yourself up on the days when your writing isn't going well. Some days the dream machine won't work. That doesn't mean it's broken.

4

Workspace

Every writer needs a place to work. It's psychologically important for a writer to have a designated workspace – be that an office, a room of your own, a favourite café, a shed in the garden, even the back seat of your car during a half-hour lunch break. The point is to designate a space that you use *only* for writing. If you have the luxury of a home office or a room of your own, then there's no limit to what you can do. Furnish it the way you want: make it suit your requirements. But whether you do or not, here are a few ideas to get you started.

1. Find a really good desk chair. So many writers have back and neck problems from slouching over a laptop all day.

2. Find somewhere you won't be interrupted. Interruptions are more than annoying; they take you out of the writing zone. If you're working from home, make sure your family understands your need for uninterrupted time. Lay down some ground rules to ensure you have some unbroken time to work – even if it's only for twenty minutes every day.

3. Turn off your phone. You may find it easier to log off the internet, too (although I quite like my little water-cooler moments on Twitter). It's all too easy to lose focus with the distraction of screens and phones. It's better to spend twenty minutes a day focusing completely on your writing than to spend hours at the computer with one eye on social media, fooling yourself you've been productive.

4. Check the temperature. Don't be too warm – warmth will make you sleepy. (Obviously, you don't want to be freezing, either. There's a limit to how much an artist should suffer.)

5. If you're working from home, try to rid your space of clutter. Clutter is often stressful and distracting, and may erode your concentration.

6. Go for a walk every once in a while, or do some stretching at your desk. I suggest every half-hour or so, or when you need five minutes' thinking time. It keeps you alert and energized as well as keeping you active.

7. Make sure you have enough natural light. Light makes a big difference to our energy levels, so for winter and on dull days, if you feel lethargic, consider getting a light box to make up for the lack of sunlight.

8. Remove any reminders from your space of any other things you have to do. Housework, letters unanswered, plants to be watered, dogs to be walked, emails from your workplace. This is your designated writing space; at least for the time you have set aside, nothing else should intrude.

9. Plan your snacks in advance. It's very easy, when working from home, either to miss meals (bad idea), or to be making toast every five minutes. Neither extreme is helpful.

10. Have a bottle of water to hand. It's easy to forget this when you're wrangling a tricky chapter, but dehydration affects your brain power and inhibits concentration.

5

Headspace

If your lifestyle makes it hard to find a designated work-space, you might benefit from a few headspace exercises. After all, if you're in the zone, your surroundings shouldn't matter. And many writers just don't have the luxury of a room of their own – they may sometimes have to write in airports, hotel rooms, railway stations. (I spent several years writing on the floor of my living room, surrounded by my daughter's toys, and with my husband watching football on TV.)

Most people have a visual imagination. A minority have very limited visual imagination, but do respond strongly to sounds, movements, tactile stimuli, even scents. Here are some shortcuts into the zone, based on sensory prompts and triggers. They may not all work for you, but you may find that one of them helps. And if this all sounds a bit too New-Agey to you, remember that creative visualization, self-hypnosis and meditation are all just ways of achieving an altered state of consciousness, which is just another way of saying 'getting into the zone'. Try it. You may surprise yourself.

1. The portable desk. Choose two objects (for fifteen years I used a candlestick and a paperweight, but they can be any-thing at all), put them in front of your laptop as you sit at your desk, or your kitchen table, or on your chosen piece of floor, or at your table in Starbucks. Handle them before you sit down to write. Get used to having them with you. Use them wherever and whenever you settle down to write – and *only* then. What you're doing is creating a *writing prompt*, which will work like any other psychological trigger, telling you: *This is your writing space – access it.* It's amazing how well this works, especially if, like me, you travel a lot, and can't get to your own desk every day.

2. The red door. This is a prompt that works best for people with strong visualization skills, and although it takes time to set up at first, it can become a useful means of getting into the zone. First, close your eyes and relax. Imagine a red door in a wall. Imagine the colour and shape of the door; the texture and colours of the wall. When you can see the door in your mind, take out the key from your pocket. Visualize the shape of the key, its weight, its texture. When you can do this, unlock the door and look inside.

Inside, is your perfect workspace. It can be anything you like: a garden, a beach, a lighthouse, a marvellous library. Go in, and spend a little time furnishing it. The better you do this, the better the visualization works. Then, when you're ready to start work, lock yourself in, using the key. Open your eyes. You should be ready.

When you've finished working, leave your space through the red door, making sure to lock it behind you. The next time you try this, it will be much quicker and easier, until eventually the visualization will only take a few seconds.

3. Identify your dominant sense. Some people (about 25 per cent) have no visual imagination. That doesn't mean they're not imaginative; it just means that, for them, other senses override the visual. If you think you're among them, identify which is your dominant sense, and tailor your prompts to suit. For instance, for a tactile memory, make sure your portable desk (if using this idea) consists of two tactile objects, rather than just visual reminders.

4. Make a writing playlist. Another useful prompt for non-visual thinkers is music. I prefer not to listen to music when I'm writing, but I like to create playlists for my characters to get me into the writing zone. Try it out: find what motivates you.

5. Build a scent library. Scent is another powerful way in which to access your creativity. The smell of rosemary has been proved to aid memory, and lavender helps with relaxation, but *any* scent can be used as a memory prompt. Just as actors often use scent to get into character, a writer can use scent as a means of getting into the zone. I use a different scent for every book I write. I use it *only* when I am writing, and before long I begin to associate it with the book, its characters and its progress. It's a great shortcut when I'm travelling, too.

6. Find your voice. Read the last chapter or page you wrote *aloud* before beginning your new day's work. (This isn't always practical in public spaces, but it really helps me find my voice.) This especially helps those who have an auditory memory, or who are affected by rhythms and cadences.

7. Find your writing uniform. We often associate being at work with the wearing of some kind of uniform. Some writers like to choose a special piece of clothing or jewellery to help them into their headspace. Rings are a common choice, but you may find that a favourite scarf, blanket or beanie can also help. The main thing is that you should *only* use it when you're writing: that way you associate it with being in the zone.

8. Create a memory book. To access certain emotions – love, happiness, grief, nostalgia and so on – put together a book of photographs or pictures that are deeply meaningful to you. It helps you access feelings that may be important in building a scene, in setting the tone, in getting into character.

9. Banish toxic influences. Many writers find that they are negatively affected by current or political affairs. If you find that you can't get current affairs out of your mind, it sometimes helps to devise a cleansing ritual – be that showering, washing your hands, casting a protective circle or burning sage before getting to work. Whatever your choice, if it works, it's all good. Like all other acts of creation, magic is just a state of mind.

10. Sometimes, whatever method you try, you find you just can't get into the zone. Don't beat yourself up about it. Dreaming on demand is an unpredictable business. Instead, go for a walk, watch a film, play with your kids, walk your dog. Remember, only a small part of the writing process actually happens at a desk. The missing piece of your story may be waiting just around the corner.

6

Time

The most common excuse people give me for not writing is not being able to find the time. But here's the thing: we all of us have the same twenty-four hours to work with. The trick is *managing the time we have* to prioritize the things we find most important. If writing is important enough to you, then you *will* find the time to write. You may have to make sacrifices, however (I mostly sacrificed ironing and dusting). Here are a few things you might like to bear in mind while you're deciding where your priorities lie.

1. Be realistic about the time you'll spend writing. Making time to write is often a challenge in a world that makes so many demands on us. But remember, you don't need to spend hours writing every day. Even if you only write 300 words every day, in a year you could already have the first draft of a novel.

2. Be mindful of what you do with your time. Is it *all* time well-spent? Chances are that some of it isn't. How long do you spend watching TV programmes you don't really like? Checking your social media? Pottering around aimlessly? Could you redirect some of that time into your writing instead?

3. Don't be afraid to enlist help. Women writers in particular are often left with the responsibilities of cooking, housework and childcare on top of their regular jobs, leaving even less time for writing. Consider delegating some of these tasks – ask a family member to cook instead, or phone for a weekly take-out – to give yourself some extra time.

4. Consider getting up an hour early to write. Or, if you're a night-owl, stay up for an extra hour. Try both, and decide which works best for you.

5. Use your lunch break to good effect. Half an hour a day, every day, adds up to a good weekly total.

6. Don't forget your regular commute. Use it, if not physically to write (not easy on a crowded Tube), to plan your writing and go over ideas.

7. Plan your writing in advance. You're far less likely to skip a day's work if you've already put the time aside.

8. Find a writing buddy. Writing is like running, or any kind of exercise: it can be motivating to share your experience with someone else.

9. If you've never tried NaNoWriMo, give it a go. (It's a yearly event, held online throughout November, during which writers from all disciplines challenge themselves to write, plan or finish a novel in a month.) The result won't be a finished novel, but many people benefit from the sense of community it brings them, and it might help you get into good habits.

10. Don't tell yourself: 'If I miss a day, I'll make it up at the weekend.' While it's true that you may have more time at the weekend, you'll end up putting yourself under unnecessary pressure, and your writing will suffer.

7

Getting Ideas

Inspiration is a mysterious concept, and one over which people too often feel they have no control. This is quite untrue; the search for ideas is an active, not a passive process. The idea that we must wait for the Muse to inspire us was invented by effete young Victorians who wanted an excuse to sit around doing nothing all day. Most of us don't have that luxury, which means forgetting about the Muse and doing some actual footwork instead.

1. Don't just sit there. Inspiration is like lightning: you can't necessarily predict *when* it will strike, but you can create the right conditions. The first is to *actively* pursue those things that may inspire you.

2. If you can, travel. Discovering new places and cultures is immensely enriching and educational. (And remember, for those of limited means, books allow you to travel, too.)

3. You don't have to go far to find ideas. There are stories all around us; the trick is learning how to see them. Train yourself to question everything you see, and to imagine the stories behind the people you meet.

4. People are fascinating. On public transport, put your phone away, take out your earplugs and observe other people. Listen to their conversations. You might hear something that sparks an idea.

5. Learn about people who are different to you. Explore the art, poetry and writing of different cultures. Look at the many diverse perspectives from which we can look at the world, and ourselves.

6. To make art, you must consume art. Go to galleries, watch plays, listen to music, play games, watch films, read books. But do it mindfully – think about what you're seeing and hearing, and think about what it makes you feel.

7. Be more aware of the world in general. That means noticing what you see, what you taste, what you smell, what you feel in all kinds of different circumstances. All these things will feed your writing if you allow it to. Write your impressions down in your notebook, or on your phone.

8. Get out of your comfort zone. Try to do things that will challenge you – whether that's training to run a marathon, or taking up a new hobby, going to a new place, or just saying hello to a stranger every day. Unexpected situations are creative, and might lead you anywhere.

9. Don't forget that you already have a library of memories. Draw from your experiences; your childhood, the key events of your own life. Not only will these give you ideas, they will also add to the emotional realism of your writing.

10. Give yourself a story prompt every day. Base it on the things you see on the way to work, or in the street outside your window. An abandoned shoe by the side of the road – what's its story? How did it get there? A woman running for a bus – where is she going? Who is she? It's surprising how often these small things can grow into something bigger.

8

Planning

There are two ways of approaching the planning of a novel. One is architectural, with a solid structural plan; the other is more fluid, allowing a degree of organic growth throughout the story. Which one you choose is up to you – and the fluid approach that works for me may not necessarily be the way that will work best for you. Both approaches, however, require a certain degree of planning.

1. Imagine you're going to take a walk through the woods. You could plan your walk in advance, using maps, looking up what plants will be flowering, checking the weather report and so on. Or you could just take your chances with whatever you happen to find on the way. In both instances, however, you need at least to know *which* woods you're heading for, and how long you're planning to spend there.

2. Sketch a map. I'm one of those writers who likes to be surprised by developments in their story – my theory is that if you can surprise *yourself*, you have more chance of surprising the reader – but it's still important to have a few key scenes or encounters in place before starting. As you develop as a writer, you may find that you want to do more or less planning as you go (much as a teacher starts off by planning their lessons in detail, then learns to plan them on the fly when they gain more experience). If you are just starting out, try putting down some basics before you start your first chapter.

3. Set the tone of your novel from the start. Though I'm not always a fan of labels, it's useful to know what camp your novel fits into: is it fantasy, or crime, or humour, or science fiction? It can be frustrating to start a novel, believing it to be one thing, only to find that it has morphed into something else over the course of fifty pages. Save yourself some editing, and get it right the first time.

4. Make sure the world of your novel is properly fixed in your mind. This applies especially if you're writing a fantasy world, but it's also true of real places. Make sure you're familiar with the terrain before rolling the tanks in.

5. Do your research. The main sweep of your plot may be fluid, but the nuts and bolts of your reality – be that the French court of Louis XV or a village in rural Kashmir – need to be as solid as possible. That means dialect, specialist vocabulary, clothing, food, historical or geographical fact-checking. You're bound to make the odd mistake, but try to avoid the obvious ones.

6. Get to know your main characters. That might mean making character lists, family trees, even sketches of your protagonist if it helps. You'll be spending a long time with these people; it pays to get to know them really well before you start your journey together.

7. Find your voice. Voice determines so much of a book: is your story best written in the first person or the third? The present tense or the past? If you're not sure, experiment. See what works best for you before you start. (More about finding your voice later.)

8. Plan your general direction. That doesn't necessarily mean knowing every step of your protagonist's journey, but it helps to have some kind of plan. Try to know what your key scenes should be, what your protagonist's aim is, what obstacles are in their way, and how their conflict should be resolved. That way you're less likely to stray off the path (and you won't have to cut hundreds of pages later, during the editorial stage).

9. Make a calendar. Make sure you know just *when* your story is happening. When you're in the throes of creativity, it's sometimes easy to forget mundane things like days of the week, weekends, moon phases and bank holidays, but those things can be important, and it's all too easy to find that you've suddenly jumped from Thursday to Sunday overnight.

10. Make sure that this is really the story you *want* to write. You're going to be spending a long time in this world, and with these characters. If by now you're not excited to start this journey, maybe you shouldn't be starting at all . . .

9

Rules, and How to Ignore Them

Beware any writer who claims to possess a set of universal rules. Rules for writers are like shoes: they exist in various sizes and styles, and one pair may fit you perfectly, while another lands you flat on your face. So by all means take an interest in rules and recommendations, but know that every single one has been broken by someone, somewhere – and often to advantage. Slavish adherence to writers' rules is as bad as pretending that there are none; and it's up to you, as you develop, to decide what works and what doesn't. Here are a few of the commonest, and why you shouldn't necessarily take them at face value.

1. **'Write what you know.'** This isn't a rule designed to limit what you write, but an invitation to encourage you to expand your knowledge. If we all restricted our writing solely to our own experience, books would be very dull indeed, and all crime writers would be in jail.

2. **'Don't break the fourth wall.'** Otherwise known as the 'Dear Reader' technique, this relates to those moments at which a character looks out from the pages and addresses the reader directly – a tricky technique, which, used clumsily,

can break the spell you're trying to weave. On the other hand, it worked just fine for Charlotte Brontë.

3. 'Show, don't tell.' There's a reason we *tell* stories, rather than *showing* the reader: a good writer will know when to do both. Too much showing (in terms of description, etc.) can sometimes lead to over-written, pretentious prose; too little can lead to the reader never being invested enough to connect with the fictional world. You need to be able to do both, at the right time and in the right place.

4. 'Write short sentences.' Though this certainly helps in terms of clarity, *always* keeping sentences short often leads to dull, turgid writing. Varying the length of sentences allows you to manage the pace of your novel and to stop it becoming predictable.

5. 'Avoid detailed descriptions.' This is one of those 'rules' that apply to a certain kind of writing, and not at all to another. The decision is entirely yours to make – and it would be a sad thing indeed if we all aimed to be the same kind of writer.

6. 'Avoid prologues.' If your book needs a prologue, feel free to include one. Just make sure it's not the boring kind that readers are likely to skip.

7. 'Don't start a book with the weather.' This is now often seen as a bit of a cliché, but there are plenty of good ways of using the weather in fiction. Perhaps, 'Don't use clichés' is a better way to put it.

8. 'Never use a verb other than "said" to report dialogue.' This is reasonable advice in the main, except that I think the only real rule is never to say 'never'. Just bear in mind that *what* a character says is usually more important than *how* they say it, and therefore needs more emphasis.

9. 'Work on one thing at a time until finished.' This is very much a personal choice. Some writers find it useful to leave a project to simmer for a while, either because they need to do more research, or because they have reached an impasse in their writing. In these cases, I think it helps to have something else to move on to; and too much pressure to finish can sometimes lead to writer's block.

10. 'Don't read the genre in which you are writing.' This advice is based on the idea that you can accidentally 'absorb' someone else's style, but if you vary your reading material (and if you're secure in your own style), this is unlikely to happen; quite the opposite, in fact: it helps to be familiar with the work of other writers in your area.

10

Research

Some books need a lot of formal research; others rather less so. But chances are that, whatever you're writing, even if it's a fantasy novel set on a distant planet in a quasi-mediaeval society of sentient lizards, you'll need to research *something*.

1. Don't be afraid to ask. When researching areas of experience, culture or expertise, your best resource is other people. If you can, talk to someone who knows more than you do, or who represents the kind of person you're writing about. Writing a police procedural? Try to befriend a helpful detective or community police officer. Writing a novel set in a school? Try to visit your local school, and find out how things are run. Writing about a particular street in London? Don't make it up: visit it, and talk to people who live there. Chances are, if you get something wrong, *someone* will point it out to you.

2. Don't just use Wikipedia. If you're researching a historical period, you'll probably need to access academic resources: libraries, records, archives, contemporary writings and journals. Facts matter: if you get them wrong, you'll pull your readers out of the story. Some of them may never return.

3. Art galleries can be an excellent resource of visual period detail. Sometimes they're the best way of researching things like food and clothing.

4. Don't make up historical or cultural details just because you think readers won't know the difference. They will, and your readers deserve respect. You may well be making things up as you go along – aren't we all? – but you're doing so within an existing framework of reality that needs to be convincing and accurate.

5. Don't mistake stereotypes for facts. Just because other people consider something to be true doesn't mean you've fact-checked it personally. You need to go the distance.

6. Try to walk in your character's shoes. If you're writing a mediaeval battle epic, try visiting a weapons museum: see what mediaeval weapons looked like, *felt* like. If you're writing a novel set in Tokyo, you need to visit Tokyo – and preferably for long enough to take in more than just local colour. (And no, looking places up online isn't enough to establish a proper sense of authenticity.) If you can't commit to your research fully, then consider writing something else.

7. Even if you're writing pure fantasy, the rules of plausibility still apply. There's no point saying: *'But it's fantasy!'* as an excuse for unbelievable, lazy, or clichéd work. Your audience owes you nothing: it's up to you to earn their trust. That's why even your mediaeval space-lizard epic can benefit from some solid research on weapons, battles, the rural economy and mediaeval social structures.

8. Don't use popular representations of places and cultures as a substitute for research. You need more than a manga collection to be able to write about Japan: more than a love of French films to write a book set in Paris.

9. You're aiming to be as authentic as possible. That means being humble, and seeking advice where required. This is especially true when you're writing about other cultures, people with different experiences, or social groups to which you don't belong. Talk to people within these groups. Listen to diverse voices. Read diverse books. Find a sensitivity reader who can help you identify if you've been culturally insensitive or inaccurate.

10. Know your limitations. If you're really having difficulty, consider the possibility that you just don't have the expertise to address the topic you've chosen. It happens. It's not your fault. Move on: you can always come back to it once you feel more confident.

PART 2

What Makes a Story?

Like buildings, stories – whatever the genre – are built from more or less the same basic materials: plots, characters, developments, themes, levels, interactions, world-building. These things may sound obvious, but these materials are essential to the building of your story, and they're worth thinking about in some detail before you start work on your first draft.

1. Characters

2. Plot

3. Subplots

4. Conflict

5. Backstory

6. Voice

7. Point of View

8. Dialogue

9. Description

10. Place

Andrea dreams of getting her novel serialized one day, if she can be bothered to write it.

1

Characters

Your characters are the people who will accompany your readers on their journey through your book. It's up to you to make these people interesting company – however marvellously crafted your plot, your readers won't care what happens next unless they are properly invested in the characters.

1. Some novels have a huge cast of characters. However, it's usually best to stick to one protagonist or main character, one or two primary characters, a handful of secondary characters, and a larger number of minor characters. Main characters need to be well-rounded and developed in detail; secondary and minor characters can afford to be less well-developed, or flat.

2. Your main character is your *protagonist*, or the *hero* of the story. You might also have an *antagonist*, who is a primary character in direct opposition to your protagonist. (That doesn't necessarily mean the *villain*, but sometimes that's the role they play.)

3. Even when you're telling the story of several primary characters at a time (e.g. Harry, Ron and Hermione), there

will be one main protagonist (in this case, Harry), without whom usually the story wouldn't be happening.

4. **If you're not sure who your protagonist is, go back to the main source of conflict.** If the conflict drives their story, the rest of the primary characters will be driven along with it.

5. **The big difference between a well-rounded character and a flat character is that a well-rounded character should have undergone some kind of change**, development or transformative experience by the end of the story. (This is often referred to as the *character journey,* or *arc.*) Without it, the character will come across as sketchy and under-developed.

6. **Secondary characters don't need dramatic character arcs**: theirs is usually just a supporting role (which doesn't mean they can't be colourful and interesting).

7. **Characters should always serve the plot in some way.** If they don't, you probably don't need them. But make sure that's not *all* they do – otherwise they'll never be convincing. Your protagonist's sidekick or best friend, to whom they tell all their secrets, needs to have at least some element or hint of a life beyond the story: another relationship, a job, a hobby, a passion.

8. **Too many characters in a story can make it hard for the reader to follow the plot.** Where a large cast of characters is necessary to the plot (e.g. in *Game of Thrones, The Lord of the Rings*) it can be a good idea to provide some kind of family tree, cast list, appendix or similar.

9. Some writers start with a story idea; others with a character. There's no right way to do this, but if you do start with the character, remember that at some point they're going to need a conflict-driven story.

10. The process of making a character come to life is called characterization. There are lots of ways to do this. (More of that later.)

2

Plot

Plot is the engine that drives your book. It's the thing that most readers stay for. Without it, not even the finest prose will keep a reader's attention; without a plot, fine writing is nothing but decoration: the paint job on a vehicle that isn't going anywhere. It therefore follows that before you start looking at the finer detailing of your story, you ensure that you have a well-tuned, fully functioning plot, which will carry your readers smoothly over the terrain of your story and deliver them safely to their destination without breaking down, hitting a plot hole, or getting stuck in quicksand.

1. Your plot is not just a series of happenings. It's the relationship between what happens in your book, and the reason *behind* what happens. A plot should take your characters (and the readers) on a kind of imaginary journey, with a departure, a continuation and a final destination.

2. You don't necessarily have to know every detail of your plot before you start. Some writers plot very meticulously; others like to leave some aspects of the journey fluid – but everyone needs to have more or less of a direction in which to aim. That means knowing the important stages of your protagonist's journey, the obstacles they will meet on the way, and the things that are likely to change them.

3. Novels often have one main plot (the main character's journey), plus a number of **subplots** (these usually concern the secondary characters), which make the journey more satisfying. Short fiction tends not to have subplots, but relies on a single driving narrative.

4. The main character's journey is usually driven by *conflict* **of some kind.** This could be inner conflict, social conflict or conflict against an enemy. That doesn't necessarily mean battles scenes or fist fights, but it does mean your protagonist needs some sort of an adversary, or some kind of adversity to overcome.

5. The more a character has at stake, the more powerful their conflict, and the more exciting and dramatic their journey. The bigger the stake (e.g. life or death, the planet, the fate of mankind), the bigger the story.

6. A plot has a beginning, a middle and an end. Nearly all stories, novels, films and plays follow the same general three-act structure. We're so used to this structure that anything that doesn't follow it usually seems wrong or off-key.

7. Part one: setting out. This stage of plot involves the introduction of the world, the main character(s) in relation to their world, and what their conflict or problem is. Here the author makes an unspoken promise to their readers: that they will deliver solutions to the conflict they have set up. It's an invitation to a journey, on which you, the author, will take them. In the standard 'hero's journey' plot structure (e.g. *Star*

Wars, The Lord of the Rings), the protagonist is often reluctant to pick up the challenge. They may need actively *persuading* to answer the call. Sometimes they may have no choice but to agree. Either way, it's about introducing a plot point that puts your protagonist under pressure, forcing them out of their comfort zone. It can be a quest, or the arrival of a personal challenge, or the introduction of an antagonist.

8. Part two: the journey. This typically takes up around two-thirds of your novel, and will include character development, interactions, problems encountered, reversals, and revelations. During this stage, narrative tension will escalate gradually, until finally it builds to a climax.

9. Part three: the destination. This may include the showdown with your antagonist, lessons learnt, conflicts resolved, and answers found (or sometimes, not). It doesn't have to be a happy ending, but your readers need to come away feeling emotionally satisfied by the conclusion of your story. Whatever you promised your readers – the lovers' reconciliation, the arrest of the murderer, the saving of the Empire – you need to deliver it here.

10. Remember that your readers want to *be taken on a journey*. They expect to get to know their travelling companions (the characters), enjoy the scenery (your world-building and description), learn new things, visit new places, and feel satisfied by the time they arrive at their destination. If by the end they've gone nowhere, learnt nothing, *felt* nothing, then you've failed in your objective.

3

Subplots

Most novels don't just have a single plotline: they usually have a variety of interleaved subplots, of greater or lesser complexity. Short fiction is less likely to include subplots, as it tends to focus on a single incident, theme or timeline. Subplots give an extra dimension to your characters and add to the believability of your story. No event in real life exists in isolation: the same is true for fiction.

1. Although your novel has only one **main plot**, it can have any number of **subplots**. Think of it like a tree: the main plot is the trunk; the subplots are the branches. These subplots will usually involve secondary characters, and will help to give life to the main story. A novel with no subplots tends to have unsatisfying or dull secondary characters, or to rely too much on 'padding out' for its length.

2. **Subplots help to make your novel more rounded and satisfying**: but they also need to be managed carefully. They need to be organically integrated into the world of your story, which means that both your fictional world and your characters need to be properly thought out.

3. **It's easy for a subplot to get out of hand**. They should always be secondary to your main plot. If you find yourself

concentrating too much energy following a subplot, then prune it down. You don't want it to drain the life out of your main narrative.

4. Make sure your subplots are always connected to the main plot in some way. Don't let them wander off, or take primary importance over your main storyline. If this happens, consider that this may be the basis for another novel, or, if necessary, strip it out completely.

5. Not all subplots need to resolve in the way your main storyline does. It's fine to leave a subplot hanging – in fact, if you don't do this where necessary, you run the risk of writing an ending that is *too* neatly tied up, and will seem unbelievable to your readers.

6. Subplots are most often connected with secondary characters: it helps give these characters a meaningful role and gives them chance to develop. But, like those secondary characters, the subplot doesn't stand alone, or rival the scale of the main narrative. In the movie *Zombieland*, the main plot is about the protagonist, Columbus, evading zombies and reaching a safe haven; in comic contrast, one of the subplots is his friend Tallahassee's desperate quest for a Twinkie. Both strands are part of the story, but only one stands alone.

7. You should be able to remove, change or add a subplot without disrupting the main story. If you can't, it isn't a subplot.

8. You can create a subplot from a couple of well-placed scenes only: they don't need to be running all the time.

9. Not every character needs a subplot. If you find yourself getting into a tangle of plots and subplots, go back to your basic story, develop it first, make it strong, then add the fine detailing later.

10. Example:

A woman is on holiday in Crete. She stumbles upon a wounded man in the mountains. He has been shot. She nurses him, and finds out that he was trying to trace a gang of criminals. His younger brother is missing. Posing as a tourist, she investigates, uncovers details of the gang, recovers the missing boy. *All this is main plot.*

The subplots: Our heroine falls in love with the wounded man after learning his story. A woman in the village is being abused by her husband, who is also one of the villains behind the kidnapping. This woman has to overcome a conflict of loyalties to help the younger brother escape. The two brothers, both strong personalities and often in conflict, are brought together by their adventure. (*By now, readers may have identified this plot as that of* The Moonspinners *by Mary Stewart.*)

The reason this works is that the main storyline is very strong and clear, and that the subplots, all of which add interest, are all firmly connected to the main plot and the primary characters, which allows them to resolve in a satisfactory manner, although any of them could, in theory, be removed without damaging the main plot.

4

Conflict

George Bernard Shaw famously said, '. . . *no conflict, no drama*', expressing the belief that all successful stories are based on conflict of one sort or another. This is sometimes misunderstood to refer to action or external conflict, but there are many different kinds of conflict, all of which can be made to be as dramatic and thrilling as you choose.

1. Conflict doesn't mean that stories have to be violent, but that the protagonist should find themselves in opposition to *something* – a person, an idea, an adversary, even an aspect of their own character.

2. Without some kind of motivating conflict, it's hard to kick-start a story. *Everyone was just fine, and stayed that way* is no way to engage a reader.

3. The easiest illustration of conflict is the 'showdown' scenario, where the conflict between the protagonist and their adversary provides the climax of the story. It's the classic Western structure, but it's also the structure of *Chocolat* . . .

4. Then there's the **Protagonist vs. The Big Opponent** (Society, Nazism, The Evil Empire), with higher stakes and greater peril, as seen in stories like *Star Wars* and *The Lord of the Rings*.

5. Other people don't need to be involved. There are some terrific Protagonist vs. Nature stories, filled with dramatic conflict.

6. Sci-fi loves the **Protagonist vs. Technology** storyline, where the big opponent is actually The Future, embodied and all-powerful.

7. Horror loves the **Protagonist vs. Supernatural Adversary** narrative (ghost, vampire, zombie plague, or other embodiment of Death), which plays the same melody on a slightly different set of keys.

8. But it isn't all about action. Quiet stories are also built with exactly the same materials. **Inner conflict** – difficult choices that must be made; the conflict caused by guilt, memories; the burden of the past; the temptation to do something dreadful – can drive a book quietly, but surely, towards a climax, with the same amount of tension and suspense as a thriller.

9. The struggle to overcome the limitations and challenges of one's own mind or body can also make for a great story. Disability, addiction, and various kinds of mental illness are all potential challenges for your protagonist to overcome.

10. If your plot is giving you trouble, one of the ways to identify where it has gone wrong is to try and identify the protagonist's conflict, and how it is driving the story. If that isn't clear to you, chances are you've lost your way, and you'll need to redraft accordingly.

5

Backstory

Backstory is what happened to your characters before the story you're currently telling. It can be central to your main story, or not at all. But given that characters are formed by events in their past, revealing these events can be useful in determining their motivations.

1. Backstory can include elements of your protagonist's background, their childhood, their upbringing, and key events in their past. Or it can contain the answer to the wider question of *why* they are there.

2. It's not always necessary for you to reveal your character's backstory. If the story is exciting enough in itself, it may simply detract from what's happening – although I would argue that *you*, the writer, should always know more about your protagonist than you choose to reveal to your readers.

3. First ask yourself what the role of your backstory is, and if your plot or your characters really need one.

4. Sometimes characters are more interesting if they don't have much of a backstory. It allows the reader to speculate if they're allowed to retain some mystery.

5. **In some cases, however, the backstory is essential, because it's central to the main character and to the plot**: for instance, in mysteries and psychological thrillers, where the past plays an important role in the unfolding of current events.

6. **Backstory can be delivered in flashback form**, but it is sometimes more rewarding to drip-feed information as the story develops.

7. **Avoid info-dumping**. You'll dump your readers, too.

8. **You should be able to handle your backstory without losing the tension from your main story**. Where long flashbacks are used, that means sustaining two connected plotlines at once, each with its own story arc. That's a delicate skill to manage – don't underestimate its difficulty.

9. **Make sure your backstory has enough tension to keep the reader's interest**. If it doesn't, you may not really need it at all.

10. **You don't need to spend pages and pages explaining why your characters are where they are**. A quick reference as part of a piece of dialogue can be as useful as an introductory chapter, and far less unwieldy.

6

Voice

Your *voice* is a combination of all kinds of different things: the way you express yourself, the things you say, the language you use, the vocabulary you're comfortable with. It's as unique to you as your fingerprints, and once you've found it, it stays with you for life. It's the expression of your personal style as a writer, and it's worth thinking about.

1. It can take a long time for a writer to find their voice. Many start off copying other writers' voices. There's no harm in this at all: it's excellent training. But ultimately, you need a voice of your own.

2. Having an authorial voice doesn't mean you can't also write from different character points of view. But it's like being an actor. Even when an actor is playing a role, some of their personality always shines through.

3. Your authorial voice is an expression of who you are: your past, your upbringing, your education, your experiences, the things you care about. As such, it will naturally change and mature as you do.

4. Your voice needs to be as natural as possible. That means being true to who you are. If you're not – if you're pretentious, or insecure, or try to be something you're not – it will show, and your voice will not be consistent.

5. Having a strong authorial voice is often a matter of confidence and maturity. That comes with time and experience. You may find that you need to experiment with different voices before you find your own – that's fine. Don't rush it.

6. Studying other voices helps. Read as widely as possible, and think about the different ways in which other writers express themselves. Each voice is subtly unique; and yet we all write about common themes. Read writers of different generations, different cultures and backgrounds. *Jane Eyre* is a coming-of-age story, but so is *The Lover*, by Marguerite Duras, and *Purple Hibiscus*, by Chimamanda Ngozi Adichie, and Jeanette Winterson's *Oranges Are Not The Only Fruit*. All of these are different depictions of the coming-of-age narrative, seen through the lens of a wide variety of different experiences.

7. Your voice is changing all the time, as you gain experience and maturity. But if it's an honest representation of who you are, it will always be recognizable as *your* voice: just as old photographs of you still look like you.

8. Some people may just not like your voice. This is not something you can change, or should feel concerned about.

9. Your voice can be as idiosyncratic or as conventional as you like. It's yours, and like the clothes you wear, you should feel completely comfortable with it.

10. Writing is like singing: some people are gifted with a naturally good voice; others need to put more work into getting there. But whether you're a natural or not, practice is essential.

7

Point of View

'Point of view' refers to the narration of a book. This could be a character (a first-person narrator, speaking from their own perspective), several characters (multiple first-person narrators), or a third-person narrator (the author, watching the action more or less closely). It's one of the ways in which you use your authorial voice to communicate the story to the reader. Some authors like their own voice to be prominent; others prefer to let their characters speak for them.

1. Think of your story as a film. Point of view (POV) is the camera. You may choose to tell your story from one or more camera angles, but however you approach it, it's worth really thinking about *how* you mean your story to come across, and how you're going to achieve this.

2. The first-person perspective is the POV shot, which puts you directly in the position of the main character. In this case, the voice needs to reflect what we know of your protagonist, reflecting their personality, their background, their age, their level of education – basically all the things that go into making a character voice unique. E.g. *'As I came in, I noticed a scent of burning in the air.'*

3. The close third person is a close shot: intimate, but not as close as a first-person narrative. This voice allows the author a high level of empathy, allowing them to look into the character's mind without actually looking at the world through their eyes. Thus: *'He entered the room, and immediately noticed the scent of smoke.'*

4. The distant third person is the long shot: it gives an objective overview, but may seem a little chilly unless you zoom in. Most third-person narratives use a combination of the close and the distant third person, which allows your camera to move in and out, giving a greater range of perspectives. E.g. *'He opened the door. The room smelt of smoke.'*

5. The second-person voice is a direct-to-camera speech (in which either the protagonist or the author speaks directly to the reader) and is less often used. That's because it can sometimes come across as annoying or contrived, unless you're writing your novel in letter or diary form or writing a pick-your-own-adventure book. E.g. *'There's smoke in the air as you enter.'*

6. When writing from a first-person perspective it's useful to consider (among other things) the character's age, background, social class, nationality, culture, education and vocabulary. All of these things are reflected in the way we express ourselves. (Use dialect with caution, though: very few people can get away with writing a whole book in authentic, convincing dialect.)

7. First- and close third-person narratives give you a great opportunity to explore a character's unspoken thoughts, to look into their past and their memories, and to follow their motivations for doing what they do.

8. The further away your camera moves from the characters, the more you reveal of the author. The closer it goes to the characters, the less you see of the author.

9. Writing in the first person means that you can't really get another perspective unless you have two cameras. I happen to like multiple first-person narrators, but it does mean working harder on separating the voices.

10. Changing perspective too often is a little like changing camera angles and positions too fast: it can be confusing for the reader. Try to keep this in mind while you're experimenting with different perspectives.

8

Dialogue

Dialogue is often the thing that less experienced authors find most difficult to master; and yet it is an essential part of the storytelling toolbox. It's often helpful in breaking up lengthy passages, speeding up the action and bringing your characters to life. It is also the way your characters express themselves and interact with each other. Ideally, every piece of dialogue in your story should reveal something – be it about the characters or the plot.

1. Adverbs are mostly unnecessary in dialogue. Plus, they often slow the pace and make it sound clunky. So, keep the adverbs for when someone says something in a really unexpected way that needs an explanation, or for comic effect.

2. You were probably taught in primary school to use a wide variety of different words for 'said'. Don't. You're not in primary school. Plus it can ruin your dialogue by taking away the focus from *what* was said, by concentrating unnecessarily on *how*.

3. Even 'he/she said' can be omitted a lot of the time. Unless you're not sure of who is speaking, you often don't really need it. Omitting the dialogue tags speeds up the dialogue and makes it sound more immediate and realistic.

4. You can also use *actions* instead of 's/he said' to direct the reader's attention towards the person who is talking. That way, your dialogue doesn't end up sounding too repetitive.

5. Listen to people around you. Everyone has their own vocal mannerisms. Apply what you hear to your characters. Use accents and verbal tics with care, though. Not everyone enjoys ploughing through pages of dialect – it's often too distracting.

6. No writer really wants to use completely authentic dialogue. People can be quite repetitive and hesitant when speaking to each other in real life. So write what *sounds* natural and fluid, not exactly what you hear.

7. Don't allow sections of dialogue to go on for more than a couple of pages. It can break up your narrative and make it feel unfinished.

8. However, don't go for too long without any dialogue at all: aim to include a short section of dialogue every half-dozen pages or so. It helps with the pacing of your book, and helps break up long, dense passages of narrative or description.

9. Dialogue is an important part of characterization. It highlights the way your characters interact with each other. And remember – what people *don't* say is often just as important as what they do.

10. Don't let your characters state the obvious. A look or a gesture can also count as character interaction, and can be more appropriate in some circumstances.

9

Description

This is the way you help your reader *experience* what's going on in your story. Sights, sounds, smells, feelings: you decide what to show them, and what to let them imagine for themselves.

1. There's no such thing as the 'right' or 'wrong' amount of description: there's only the right amount for *you*. Some authors linger lovingly over description; others feel that it slows down the narrative, and prefer to leave most of the details to the reader's imagination. It depends on what kind of book you're writing – a heavily plot-based thriller may indeed suffer from too much fine detailing – but to draw the reader into your world, it often helps to give them a sensory access-point or two.

2. Having said that, don't overdo it. The reader wants to be immersed in a story, not drowned in words.

3. Don't describe the obvious. 'The sun was shining brightly in the sky' is both obvious (where else would it be shining?) and dull. More effective would be to describe the sun shining on water, or glass, or to have your protagonist feel the heat of the sun on their neck.

4. Don't just describe what your characters see or hear. Use all of your senses, and theirs.

5. Don't try to describe *everything*. Concentrate on well-chosen details – a scent, a colour, a shape, a sound, an object, a feeling. Pick what's interesting to you. Leave the rest to the reader's imagination.

6. Descriptive passages need to have a purpose. They should either serve the plot, or the atmosphere, or the world-building, or the overall mood of the piece. If a passage doesn't serve a purpose, it's just pointless decoration. Kill it.

7. Never use description as padding to improve your word count. It is best integrated into some other aspect of the narrative, otherwise it can feel clunky or bolted-on.

8. Description tends to slow down the narrative. If you're aiming to speed up the narrative pace, go easy on the descriptions. If you're wanting to slow things down, introduce more detail.

9. When introducing a new character, tell your reader the important stuff straightaway. Otherwise, the reader will already have built up their own mental picture of the person, which you may later contradict.

10. It's generally not a good idea to go into too much detail when describing characters. Think of what you'd notice first about them. What's their most striking feature? Do their clothes contribute to the reader's sense of what they're like? Remember, you're not painting a picture, you're trying to create a quick sketch that reveals something about their personality.

10

Place

One of the most important elements of any story is the author's portrayal of their world. It's the part of the story that makes the reader feel as if they're really included in the story you're telling – and it's the thing that will make them want to return. This means creating a sense of place, or if we're speaking of worlds other than our own (fantasy worlds, historical or futuristic scenarios), world-building.

1. World-building isn't really about *building* worlds. It's about portraying the world of your story in a believable way, using building-blocks from your own experience and research. It's also about how your protagonist interacts with *their* world: a knight in your mediaeval battle epic is likely to have a very different world picture and knowledge base than, for instance, a nun or a peasant.

2. The better we know our own world, the better we are at representing fictional versions of it. Everywhere you go, every country you visit or culture you experience can be used to expand your cultural knowledge and to improve your ability to imagine new worlds. That goes for fantasy worlds as well: everything potentially goes to feed your fiction.

3. Most of us don't know much about our world, except the parts of it we have seen. The same is true of fictional characters: all they can really know is their own limited world within the larger one. (Some authors, especially of sci-fi and fantasy, tend to forget this.) For historical scenarios, this can be especially true: most characters have no experience of anything outside their own immediate geographical location.

4. It's a good idea to remember this when creating fantasy worlds, which can sometimes otherwise come across as lacking in **cultural, racial, geographical and meteorological diversity**. Dream big. Our world contains a multitude of species, cultures, customs, landscapes, climates. Why shouldn't yours?

5. A lot of second-rate sci-fi and fantasy suffers from the 'Earth-type planet' trope (in which 'Earth-type' means something like 'a gravel pit in Oxfordshire, on a sunny Wednesday afternoon in spring'). That's not all Earth has to offer. It's not even all Oxfordshire has to offer.

6. The same is true of the different races living in your fantasy world. Even though they may not relate to Earth races, the old 'dwarves are greedy, orcs are aggressive, elves are spiritual' tropes are a reflection of real-world racism. We can all do better than this.

7. Good world-building does not mean a vast info-dump of descriptions and maps at the beginning of a book. There's no point losing your readers in detail before your story even begins. A small, well-placed detail – the shape of an eating utensil, the name of a local fruit – can sometimes achieve more than a whole raft of footnotes and diagrams.

8. We don't usually experience our own world through maps. Consider the usefulness of things like climate, vegetation, agriculture, wildlife, the economy, political regimes, social infrastructure, dialect, food, cities, belief systems, etc. to introduce readers to a place or world.

9. It's useful to look at the ways in which *we ourselves* experience our world. Look at the relative importance of things like food and language when entering a culture. These things can sometimes determine how confidently we explore it.

10. The best-drawn fantasy worlds are the ones that are believable and familiar as well as being exotic and strange. That doesn't mean we can't have fantasy species, but we need to be made to believe in their physicality, too. (A well-placed pile of dragon or unicorn scat can go a long way in doing this. And to paraphrase Terry Pratchett, when writing a fantasy city, you should always know how the drains work.)

PART 3

Shall We Dance?

Writing a story is something like inviting the reader to dance with you. You need to be inviting, to establish a mood, to set the rhythm, to play the music you think they'll like. Then, it's up to you to guide them through the dance without missing a beat, or losing them, or treading on their toes.

1. The First Line
2. Pacing and Tension
3. Flashbacks
4. Chapters
5. Creating Atmosphere
6. Themes
7. Beats
8. Style
9. Imagery
10. The Ending

He wore a shovel hat, a Norfolk jacket,
Tobi trousers and Chukka boots.
Beside him walked his faithful Alaskan
Malamute. [note 2 self: GOOGLE THESE]

1

The First Line

Beginning a story in the right way, and in the right place, is the secret to taking your readers with you. If you don't engage them in the first few pages, they may not follow you at all. This is especially true of short fiction, but even with a novel, you need to entice the reader. A strong and evocative opening will do that better than any number of cover quotes: most readers skim the first page of a book before they decide to buy it, so think of your first line as your chance to set out your stall for your readers.

1. Beware of what creative-writing tutors refer to as 'hooks'. Sure, it's important to grab your reader's attention as quickly as you can, but it's important to do it in a way that doesn't end up with the reader feeling cheated. I'm all for an arresting opening sentence, but make sure you consider tone. An over-flashy or over-dramatic opening can sometimes end up sounding like a cheap device to attract attention, and may ultimately alienate your reader.

2. Ideally, your reader should be drawn into your story before they even realize it's happening. It doesn't automatically have to be in the very first sentence, although if they're not with you by the end of the first couple of pages, they're unlikely to stay the distance.

3. **One way of drawing the reader in is to introduce them to a character they're likely to find interesting or relatable.** That doesn't mean a massive info-dump: a well-chosen detail or two might be enough to intrigue them and make them want to read on.

4. **Another way is to present your reader with an interesting thought, unanswered question or piece of information that they may never have considered before.** They'll read on to find out its significance, after which it's up to you to reel them in with well-drawn characters and an engaging story.

5. **Or you can start off with a bang.** Iain Banks does this very well – he often surprises his audience into the story with a series of startling, sometimes shocking opening sentences that hook the reader immediately. But this bravura method only works if the whole novel is in a similar register. If you're writing a quiet, reflective story, you'll have to start it off in a quiet, reflective way. That doesn't mean sacrificing tension or mystery. It means you'll have to be more subtle. There's a reason *Jane Eyre* begins with the line: '*There was no possibility of taking a walk that day,*' rather than, '*It was the day my grandmother exploded.*'

6. **Whichever way you choose to start, don't start with something the reader is likely to skip, whilst waiting for something good to happen.** Give them the good stuff right away. That means delivering as little background or factual information as possible: unless they are invested in your story and your characters, they won't care enough to assimilate it.

7. **Plunging your readers into a new and exciting world can be as dramatic as engaging them with a dramatic incident.**

If you can create a world in the first paragraph that your readers really want to explore, you're already on the right track.

8. You don't have to wait for the perfect opening scene to come to you before beginning your story. Lots of writers work on later scenes as they wait for their opening scene to find them.

9. It could be that the best way for you is simply to write your way into your story. Don't worry too much about the quality of what you're writing, or the story you're telling: just write about your protagonist, their thoughts, their comings and goings. I think of this as the scaffolding stage: support for the thing you're building. At some point you'll find your opening scene, and with it, your first line. When you reach it, just get rid of everything you wrote previously – take down the scaffolding – and you're off!

10. Keep thinking about what's most important in your story. Is it a character, an incident, a relationship? Whatever it is, it should feature, however obliquely, in your story's opening. You're taking the reader on a journey. You should at least hint at where you're going.

2

Pacing and Tension

Once you've thrown out your first line, you need to make sure your readers will stay with you till the end of your journey together. One of the principal ways to do this is through correct handling of pacing and tension.

The pacing of a novel is the way in which your readers will experience their journey through your narrative. This isn't necessarily about a book being a 'quick read' or otherwise; nor is it about a story being exciting or not. Some books are fast-paced, while others rely on a slower build-up to the climax; but, properly handled, either can be satisfyingly filled with drama and tension.

1. The overall pace of a novel can be faster or slower according to what the author is trying to achieve. Whichever it is, the pace should vary at different moments throughout the book. Variety is the key here: a book that is very fast-paced throughout will end up being just as wearing and dull as one that never revs up at all.

2. We tend to think of thrillers and action and adventure stories as being fast-paced, but actually, good pacing is less about speed and more about the correct managing of *tension*. Keeping tension in a story is like flying a kite: sometimes you have to pull the string (increase the tension) and sometimes you need to let it loose (decrease the tension), otherwise it won't fly properly.

3. In practical terms, that means including slower, more contemplative or humorous scenes to break the tension once it reaches a peak. Your readers need time to breathe.

4. It can help create tension if you introduce a deadline of some kind into the story. The need for your protagonist to complete a task within a set time limit (to prove the innocence of the accused before they go to the electric chair; to find the kidnap victim before the killer finishes them off; to win the heart of the heroine before she marries the Wrong Man) can really contribute to the suspense.

5. Tension doesn't have to be about peril or action or suspense: it can be quiet and character-driven, too. And sometimes the slowness of a developing scene helps ramp up the tension, making the readers even more invested in the pay-off.

6. In an action-based sequence, dialogue can slow down the pace. In a slow, descriptive scene, dialogue makes things move faster.

7. Much of the secret of pacing is about the timing of key events in your narrative. It's useful to space these out evenly, as well as allowing for some moments of decreased tension in order to create a contrast, and to allow your readers time to assimilate new developments.

8. It's hard to get your reader to care about a character in peril if you haven't introduced your character properly.

That means showing them in a more relaxed context before you put them in danger. The more the reader already likes and identifies with the character, the more likely they are to feel invested in their fate.

9. When you're building tension, you need to make sure that every tension spike escalates from the previous one. You wouldn't follow up a scene about a vampire clown with one about a larger-than-usual spider.

10. Whammies and surprises in a plot work very like the punchlines to jokes: the better or longer the build-up, the more effective the whammy. However, you need to make sure that the whammy is worth the build-up of tension; there's nothing worse than a climax turning into a damp squib.

3

Flashbacks

Flashback is a technique that allows an author to deliver more backstory. Colm Toibin advises authors to avoid flashbacks completely. I don't think you have to, although they are not always easy to handle. If badly written, they can be clunky, and they're often challenging to incorporate into a plot but, well-handled, they can work, and can serve to add an extra dimension to your narrative.

Here are a few things to bear in mind:

1. Flashbacks are ways of revealing key moments in a character's backstory, including from the point of view of the protagonist.

2. Knowing about a character's past is often the key to understanding them. A flashback from their perspective can really help bring them to life and provide insights about their behaviour.

3. A well-placed flashback can be a good way of introducing a location, a secondary character or a recurring theme.

4. Flashbacks don't have to be long. They can vary in length between a whole book and a single sentence.

5. Flashbacks can really help build suspense, by allowing the writer to start the story at a point of maximum tension, then looking back at how you arrived there. The whole of Daphne du Maurier's *Rebecca* is basically a long flashback. So is Vladimir Nabokov's *Lolita*.

6. You don't need the equivalent of the wibbly screenwipe or the shift to black-and-white to move to a flashback. There are many different ways to enter a flashback situation (diary pages, photographs, memories triggered by plot events).

7. Real people remember things all the time through sounds, scents, impressions. Your characters can do the same.

8. You can convey a lot about a character just by a single reference to the past – a childhood memory, a remembered habit, a sense-impression; all these can trigger memories.

9. Or you can plunge right into the past and reproduce a chapter-long episode in all its remembered detail.

10. But make sure you're not slowing the plot down for no reason. Make sure any flashback activity remains relevant to what's happening in your story's present. And longer incursions into your character's backstory need their own story arc in order to keep the reader's attention. (This is especially true in novels built on two timelines, where both stories need to intersect and climax at more or less the same time.)

4

Chapters

Most authors (though not all) choose to divide their books into chapters. It makes it easier for the reader to assimilate the text, as well as allowing for natural breaks in the narrative.

1. There are no hard and fast rules about chapter length: it depends on the type of novel, the rhythm and pace of the narrative and the author's personal preferences, but modern readers often seem to prefer relatively short chapters (5–15 pages in length).

2. Some books have no chapters at all. This can sometimes make it difficult for the reader to find a natural place to stop reading. That may sound like a good thing – I mean, you *want* them to keep going, right? – but in fact, it can slow down the overall pace and make it harder to concentrate.

3. Nineteenth-century novels often included detailed chapter headings, explaining what was going to happen in the next section. Nowadays this approach seems old-fashioned, and most authors choose either shorter headings, or just numbered chapters.

4. Chapters can be used to control the pace of a novel by introducing natural breaks (which can serve either as a break from the action, or as cliffhangers to build suspense).

5. Chapter breaks are also useful when changing character POV, or when moving from one scene to another.

6. Chapters help to establish the rhythms of a novel, which is why it's often useful to keep your chapters more or less the same length.

7. It can also be quite effective, for the sake of making an impact, to occasionally include a really short chapter. This breaks the rhythm and can therefore be used to showcase a crucial plot development, or to build suspense. (In *Something Wicked This Way Comes*, Ray Bradbury has a chapter consisting of a single line, marvellously ominous in its brevity: '*Nothing much else happened, all the rest of that night.*')

8. Some authors like to use quotes at the beginning of a chapter. There's nothing wrong with this, but be aware of any potential usage costs you might incur, especially if you're using song lyrics, which can be *very* expensive, and which most publishers expect the author to pay for.

9. The first and last lines of any chapter are the ones likely to have the greatest impact on the reader. Make them count.

10. Every chapter or scene should have an arc of some kind: you should be able to chart your character's starting-point and finishing-point. If no progress has been made, nothing learnt, no ground covered, then maybe rethink your chapter.

5

Creating Atmosphere

Atmosphere – or *mood* – is the part of your story that is neither plot, nor theme, nor character, but which, if you can create it, makes your readers feel they are breathing the air of your fictional world and sharing it with your characters. Atmosphere is the difference between just *watching* the story unfold and being part of the experience.

1. Think of it as the soundtrack of a movie. Soundtracks enable us to create feelings, moods, suspense and more – except that this is a soundtrack that also engages the other senses, too.

2. It can be built through descriptions, of course, but also through vocabulary choices, dialogue, imagery and the pacing of your narrative.

3. To be really effective, it has to be properly integrated into the narrative. If you think of it as 'padding', chances are you're not doing it properly.

4. Creating atmosphere shouldn't slow down your narrative (unless you want it to, of course). You can do a hell of a lot with a few (well-chosen) words.

5. When setting a scene, it's a good idea to ask yourself what atmosphere you're trying to build. Menacing? Tranquil? Idyllic? Romantic? Tense? Adjust your style accordingly. You don't want to be using violent imagery if you're trying to paint a tranquil scene.

6. Sentence structure helps a lot when you're building atmosphere. Short sentences speed up the pace. Long, complex sentences with multiple sub-clauses and numerous ideas tend – like this one – to slow it down.

7. The weather is often used to create atmosphere within a scene. But it can often lead to clichéd writing. Use it with caution. If something has been done before, consider not doing it.

8. To change the atmosphere of a scene, you can use a physical sensation (scent, taste, touch, etc.) to trigger feelings and memories in your protagonist. All this adds to creating a sense of immediacy and engagement for the reader.

9. If you want your readers to feel confused or overwhelmed, then pile on the sense-impressions. If you want them to have a more relaxed ride, then introduce them to your world one well-drawn detail at a time.

10. Sometimes, it helps to subvert expectations. It's sometimes more shocking to have a bright and cheery soundtrack against a horrific scene instead of the usual ominous chords (think of the scene in Kubrick's *A Clockwork Orange* which uses Rossini's upbeat *Thieving Magpie* as the soundtrack to ultra-violence). In the same way, it can be nice to mix up your sense-impressions to create a different kind of mood. Instead of your detective smelling blood at the crime scene, imagine how you could vary the mood by having them smell flowers, bacon, petrol, grass.

6

Themes

Your *themes* are the ideas underlying your plot. *Pride and Prejudice*, for example, is a romantic comedy, but some of the *themes* are: first impressions, hypocrisy, family, deceit, romantic relationships. Most authors don't plan their themes in the same way that they plan their story or characters, but all the same it's useful to try to identify where the themes of your story lie.

1. The strongest and most relatable themes are universal: love, death, revenge, desire, beauty, grief, courage, jealousy, family – things that readers from every culture and time will recognize.

2. There's no limit to the number of themes you can explore in a novel, but like characters, it helps to keep to just a few major themes and a larger number of secondary themes.

3. Themes should underpin a story: giving the reader something to think about after the story has been told.

4. Sometimes (but not always) a theme delivers a message or moral: for example, *Pride and Prejudice* (again). Theme: *relationships*. Moral: *you can't have a long-lasting relationship* *without honesty and mutual respect.* In this case the story presents the readers with numerous examples of different relationships, proving the point by example.

5. Themes can be delivered by direct example, but also through reinforcement throughout the story. For instance, if your main theme is courage, then courage should form the basis of your protagonist's development, inform his relationships, and help drive the plot.

6. Mood can make a contribution to theme, although they are not the same thing. But if one of your main themes is death, then you'd expect the mood of your novel to reflect it, through colours, or perhaps through your choice of imagery.

7. A *leitmotiv* is often associated with the development of a theme. (Originally a musical term, the word refers to a short and recurring musical phrase.) In literature it's any recurring detail (e.g. the colour red, the taste of chocolate, the idea of coming home) that reinforces a central theme.

8. When developing your own themes, it helps to look at art critically, and to try to identify and think about the themes of the books, films and plays you experience.

9. Themes are often closely linked to your characters. If in doubt, ask yourself: *What does my protagonist believe in most? (Friendship? Courage? Love? God? Duty? Patriotism? Family?)* The answer will almost certainly be one of the main themes of your story, and is likely to be reflected in their behaviour.

10. If you can't clearly identify the main themes of your novel, it's worth revisiting your plot and characterization. It could be that they need reinforcing.

7

Beats

Beats in fiction, as in music, are what we use to keep the pace or tempo of a story going. In storytelling, as in dancing, keeping time is essential. Miss a beat, and you're likely to tread on your partner's toes.

1. In a novel, your beats are *the main plot points* that drive your story. You should be able to write each one down as a one-line summary. For example:

A stranger arrives in town.
Mr Bingley invites the girls to a dance at his home.
Elizabeth Bennett meets Mr Darcy for the first time.

2. These driving beats are normally followed by reactions from characters, development, suspense, dialogue and all the other ingredients that help to build your story.

3. Example:

Beat: *A stranger arrives in town.*

Reaction: The Bennett girls are excited, because the stranger is a wealthy single man.

Development: We learn more about the Bennett family. Mr Bennett seems disinclined to get to know the interesting stranger.

Beat: *Mr Bingley invites the girls to a dance at his home.*

Reaction: The Bennett girls and their mother are very excited. Elizabeth remains aloof.

Development: We see the girls at the party, and learn more about them. Elizabeth, especially, has strong ideas about the kind of man she's looking for.

Beat: *Elizabeth Bennett meets Mr Darcy for the first time.*

Reaction: He is rude: she is unimpressed.

4. **The reactions and developments that follow a beat** help build anticipation and provide a context for the next beat.

5. That's why **whatever medium you're writing for** (film, novel, theatre, short story) it's important for the beats of a story to be regular and well placed, with plenty of space for reactions and developments.

6. **With experience, you may well find you develop your sense of timing.** But whether you plan ahead in detail or allow your plot to grow organically, at some point, you'll have to go through your story – be it at the planning stage, or later, at the rewriting stage – to make sure your beats are in the right place.

7. **Try drawing a diagram of your story,** marking the beats and reactions along the way. It should become very clear if there's a point at which too many things all happen at once, or if the story slows down longer than it should.

8. **Or think of your beats as stepping-stones across a river.** For obvious reasons, don't leave it too long before dropping the next one.

9. You may have heard the term 'second-act slump'. This applies mostly to films, but is equally true of some novels. It refers to the saggy bit in the middle of a story, where the plot can lose momentum. This is usually either because the author is juggling too many subplots, or because they have failed to manage the tension correctly.

10. If you think your plot is suffering from second-act slump, go back to your story diagram. Make sure the beats are in the right place. Make sure that each beat shows the tension mounting.

8

Style

Style is a combination of your own authorial voice and the techniques you use to express it. It's up to you how much you think about it – some authors write very naturally; others do a lot more stylistic planning and refining of style – but here are some things to consider.

1. The tone of your authorial voice, when it comes to delivering your message. Obviously, if you're writing a romantic comedy, your tone can afford to be light-hearted; if you're writing a noir thriller you'll need a different kind of tone.

2. Your sentence structure and length determine how your reader experiences your story. Make sure to vary sentence length – short sentences for a faster pace, longer ones to slow it down – to make sure it never gets boring.

3. Description is the way you ensure how your reader sees your world. Make sure your reader never gets bored, or wishes the plot would move faster. That means delivering just enough detail to bring your world to life, but not enough for your reader to want to skip passages in order to get to the good bits.

4. Your choice of vocabulary can be an important part of your style. That means considering (among other things) the sound of the words you use, their meaning, how they chime with the themes of your book, and whether they reflect the tone of your story.

5. Style is not just about creating beautiful sentences. **Language can be as beautiful or as ugly as the story requires.** Both can have an impact.

6. Your style should reflect what you're trying to achieve when it comes to your reader. Do you want them to hold their breath? Laugh? Cry? Get angry? Whatever it is, make sure you know *what* you're trying for, and how you want to make it happen.

7. A simple style of language can be just as effective as a complex vocabulary choice. With complicated language, there's always the chance that you might end up losing your reader.

8. Style is less about tricks and technique and more about general attitude. Be confident in your own style, and let it reflect your personality.

9. Make sure you're not being repetitive. Everyone has stylistic tics – tricks or phrases that they use too often. Identify your unwanted mannerisms, and make sure you get rid of them, either in the first draft, or at the rewriting stage.

10. Whatever your style, keep it consistent. You need your reader to feel that, wherever the plot takes them, they're going to be in safe hands.

9

Imagery

Imagery is a collective term used for aspects of (often visually) descriptive language, which includes a number of literary devices, such as similes, metaphors, etc. Basically, it's the colour palette in a writer's box of tricks. Its purpose is to help the reader visualize the scene you're describing, preferably in a new and interesting way.

1. Under-use of imagery tends to make for dull, flat prose. Over-use of it can make for overwritten, pretentious prose. Avoid both, if possible.

2. Never use imagery just for the sake of it, or because you think it's clever. Like anything else you write, it has to earn its keep.

3. A single striking image is often enough to illuminate a whole passage. Think about quality, rather than quantity.

4. If you're writing from a character's point of view, choose the image they're likely to use. There's no point in giving an image about fishing to a character who lives nowhere near water, or a visual image to a character who is blind from birth.

5. Avoid clashing images, unless you're going for a particular kind of contrasting effect. For instance, if your scene is filled with food imagery, it's probably not a good idea to add a simile about computers.

6. It's usually better to focus your imagery on something central to the scene, rather than on peripheral details.

7. Try to avoid images you've encountered many times before. They're usually not interesting enough to deserve your attention (or the reader's).

8. Always think about what your imagery means, and what visual it's likely to convey to the reader. It's easy, especially with extended pieces of imagery, to be accidentally hilarious.

9. Good imagery doesn't have to be complicated. What it has to do is convey something new to the reader.

10. Use your imagery to reinforce the overarching themes of your story. As an example, this quote by Angela Carter from *The Bloody Chamber*: '*His wedding gift . . . a choker of rubies, like an extraordinarily precious slit throat,*' warns us that the relationship she's describing is About To Go Terribly Wrong.

10

The Ending

The ending of your story is your last chance to connect with your reader. It's where, if they've enjoyed the dance, you exchange phone numbers and promise to meet again soon. Just *how* you do this will determine whether they're likely to read your work again, so it's up to you, having kept them with you so far, to make sure they leave your story feeling satisfied. That means thinking hard about the tone of your ending: think what mood it's going to convey, think what kind of images you're going to leave your readers with. It doesn't have to be a conventionally *happy* ending. *Wuthering Heights* ends with the graves of Catherine and Heathcliff, but nevertheless manages to convey a mood of tranquillity, as well as the promise of new life. Here are a few things to think about as you're planning your ending.

1. There are lots of ways to end a story, depending on what kind of a story it is. **There's the 'happy-ever-after' ending,** in which you wave goodbye to your characters for ever.

2. In an ongoing series, there's the 'things-ended-up-okay-*for-a-while*' ending, which hints at a continuation.

3. Then there's the 'Scooby-Doo' ending, which finishes on a joke, to relieve all the built-up tension.

4. And the 'long-shot' ending, where the camera pans away into the landscape, creating the illusion of tranquillity.

5. Whatever kind of a story it is, it should end in some kind of resolution: a victory, the reuniting of the lovers, the solution to the puzzle, the end of the journey.

6. It doesn't have to answer *all* the reader's questions, but it shouldn't cheat them, either.

7. This should be a quiet time for your characters or, at least, a period of rest.

8. Cliffhanger endings, even in a series, rarely satisfy completely; with novels, the readers are often likely to turn off.

9. The ending should release tension, not rack it up. That way the climax of your story is all the more satisfying.

10. However you decide to end it, your story should always deliver what you promised your readers. They need to walk away feeling emotionally satisfied, and with something new to think about.

PART 4

Characterization

Remember to make your
minor characters distinctive.

1

Growing Your Characters

A character who doesn't grow in some way is doomed to remain two-dimensional. You can get away with a certain number of two-dimensional *secondary* characters, but if you want your protagonist to sit up and breathe, they must be capable of growth, development and change. The phrase 'hero's challenge' or 'hero's journey' refers to a specific kind of mythic story structure but, arguably, all protagonists in fiction need to go on some kind of a journey.

This doesn't have to be a 'challenge' in the classic style (e.g. Frodo's quest to destroy the One Ring, Luke's call to rescue Princess Leia, Sherlock Holmes being called upon to solve a murder), although those are pretty typical examples. It's really more about where your protagonist stands at the beginning of the book, and deciding where they need to be at the end (e.g. *Persuasion*: Anne Elliot, disappointed in love and resolved to be an old maid at the beginning of the novel, reunited with her lover by the end of it). In some cases both the 'journey' and the 'challenge' are entirely internal, and are about the character's own self-discovery within the narrative.

Either way, if you're having difficulty identifying your protagonist's challenge, it helps to ask yourself: *'Where is my protagonist now? What do they want?'* Here are a few things to think about if you think your protagonist needs to grow.

1. Make a plan of your character's arc. Decide from the outset how much you need your protagonist to change, and what you need them to become. What's their aim? To fall in love? To overcome an enemy? To learn a difficult life lesson? To change from a comfort-loving young hobbit to the saviour of Middle-earth? Either way, they should have a journey – the longer the journey, the more dramatic the story – and you should have some idea of what kind of challenges your plot is going to throw at them to enable them to fulfil their potential.

2. People grow and change through contact with other people. Your characters can do the same. At the end of every scene, try asking yourself: *What has my protagonist learnt from this? How has it affected them?*

3. Characters grow more real as readers learn more about them. Keep your readers interested by revealing new details about your protagonist throughout the story. Make sure you, the author, know at least these things: what relationship they had with their parents; what they're most afraid of; what they love; what they most want out of life. That way you'll be able to understand the decisions they take, and the mistakes they make.

4. People show different facets of their personality in different circumstances. The more varied your protagonist's experiences, the more chance you have to reveal how they respond.

5. Everyone is shaped by their past, their parents and their upbringing. Your protagonist is no exception.

6. Everyone – heroes and villains included – needs someone, or something, to love. If you find yourself needing to humanize a character, try to work out who or what they love – a relative, a lover, a friend, a dog or cat, an ideal, a physical object or souvenir of something important to them – it will help. Even the amoral Alex in *A Clockwork Orange* loves music – and that immediately gives him another dimension, and a longer, more interesting arc as he faces losing what he loves most.

7. Remember, your plot is a vehicle that takes your protagonist on a journey. That means the *plot* is your main chance to reveal things about your characters. If the journey hasn't given your characters the chance to learn new things about themselves or about their world, the journey wasn't worth going on, and you may need to rethink your plot.

8. Small details matter. You can learn a lot about a character from little things: their habits, their likes and dislikes, how they eat, even how they dress. Just a few, well-chosen details are enough to make a secondary character stand out.

9. Look at your protagonist through the perspective of other characters in your story. No one ever sees anyone in exactly the same way. Use the opportunity to show different facets of your protagonist by putting them into situations of intimacy, conflict, stress, and interactions with other characters.

10. Although *you* may like a character and identify with them from the start, remember that your readers need to get to know them before they can feel the same way. That means you need to work actively to create sympathy, liking or some kind of a human connection.

2

Main Characters

Because you will usually have only one or two main characters, it's essential for them to stand out as boldly as you can make them. That means creating fully rounded individuals, capable of inspiring real feelings in your readers. It's worth spending time on thinking this out: the more real your characters are to *you*, the more likely they are to convince your readers.

1. Your protagonist is the person in your story who drives the narrative. In some cases where a relationship is central to your storyline, you can have two protagonists of equal importance; but even in a love story, this isn't necessarily the case.

2. You need to know enough about your protagonist to predict what they might do in different sets of circumstances, and why. This may not always be something that makes it into your story, but it's important that you, the author, should know.

3. Beware of identifying too much with your protagonist. It's good to have things in common with them, but you also need to keep some objectivity and some awareness of their flaws. Some authors write their protagonists as idealized versions of themselves, which makes it hard for a reader to believe in them.

4. Don't expect to know everything about your protagonist straightaway. As with a real person, getting to know a fictional person takes time. If you find yourself struggling, remind yourself of what you most need to know: where they are from, what they most want, and what their journey represents for them.

5. There should be some reminder of your protagonist in every scene, even when they're not physically around. That could mean discussion of them by secondary characters, visual reminders of what they stand for, and an awareness of what they're doing elsewhere, while the scene unfolds.

6. If your protagonist is also the narrator of the story, it's less easy to get the chance to see them through the eyes of other characters. You can compensate for this by introducing more scenes in which your protagonist interacts with others, giving an opportunity for dialogue between them.

7. You don't always have to like your protagonist. But you do need to feel interested in them. If you find that your protagonist isn't as interesting as your villain, or your secondary characters, that's probably because you haven't given them a convincing character flaw, or the opportunity to make mistakes.

8. Don't write a protagonist that you want to fall in love with. Even if you're writing a romance, you need some objectivity. Otherwise your characters will come out very flat and dull. (This is particularly true of men writing women characters – more of that later.)

9. Try to think of your protagonist as a real person. Imagine them in as many different situations as possible.

10. A main character should never do anything merely to serve the plot. However important it might be to get your character from one place to another, you need a reason other than, 'I wanted them to do this.' Otherwise all your characterization will fail, and your living character will lie down and go flat again.

3

Secondary and Minor Characters

Every novel needs secondary and minor characters – parts that don't have the depth of characterization as the main character. Because they won't have the same depth as your main character, it's important for them to stand out and be distinct among your supporting cast.

1. Some of them may appear only once: a waitress, a traffic policeman, a passer-by. These are your *minor characters*, the equivalent of extras in a film. These people are entirely flat, and it's fine in most cases for them to be there simply to serve the plot.

2. *Secondary characters* **are more fleshed-out,** and exist to support the main character and give them someone to bounce off – they're like the supporting roles in a movie.

3. It's easy for secondary characters to feel rather *too* supportive of the protagonist, with no agency of their own. You need to keep the balance. Don't allow your secondary characters to slip into generic roles – the Love Interest, the Best Friend, the Nemesis – ideally, they should still have some hint of a life outside of their relationship with your protagonist.

4. Having said that, it's also easy to fall into the trap of trying to make them too complex, thereby upsetting the balance. But introducing even *one* detail of their life will help make them believable – how many best friends in fiction seem to have no family, no past, no partner, no life at all outside their friendship with the protagonist?

5. With secondary and minor characters, it's often best to start small. Start by giving a new character just one identifying feature: a physical feature, a mannerism, an item of clothing.

6. We never notice everything about a person at first glance. Make the one thing you mention count. In the case of a minor character, make it something that bears repeating: e.g. *Man in White Suit.* It serves as a kind of trigger that allows the reader to identify the character quickly.

7. For instance, your hero's in hospital. You need a nurse character with a speaking part. You could look at body type, race, personality, attitude. But whatever you choose, **keep it short.** For example: '*He awoke to find himself in hospital. A cheery nurse with pink hair explained the situation.*'

8. Make it something that stands out visually. Most people remember visual markers best.

9. If your protagonist interacts with them more than once, then you can add more detail. E.g. '*The pink-haired nurse looked tired.*'

10. If they keep appearing, you might want to give them a name, or even add more details. *'The pink-haired nurse was called Mike.'* (Bet you thought that nurse was going to be a woman, didn't you? Keep challenging your readers' prejudices.)

4

Flawed Characters

No one likes a person with whom they have no connection. And no one believes in a person who is entirely without character flaws. Because we all have flaws of our own, we often find 'perfect' characters dull and unbelievable. As a rule, we feel more closely connected with characters who struggle. Our flaws – and how we cope with them – are part of what makes us human, and if you want your characters to appear complex and three-dimensional, then you need to give them believable flaws as well as believable qualities.

1. The flaws you give your character should be unconnected to their physicality. Giving your beautiful heroine a slightly bigger nose than average, or making her a bit clumsy, doesn't count as a character flaw.

2. Just how flawed you make your character is up to you, but even when writing a deeply damaged or morally ambivalent character, it's always possible to create a level of empathy. The trick is in the way you portray their *awareness* of their flaws, and whether or not they're trying to overcome them. We always relate better to people who know their own weaknesses, and are struggling to overcome them.

3. Bear in mind that real people aren't always consistent. They are capable of doing both very good and very bad things in different circumstances. Your job is to make that inconsistency make sense, and to always know *why* your character makes any particular decision.

4. It's far easier for the reader to empathize with a character if they can understand why they do the things they do. Even if the character doesn't know it themself, *you* should know, and convey it somehow to your readers.

5. People are the product of their childhood, background, upbringing and past experiences. The more we know about these things, the less we are likely to think of someone as 'naturally' good or bad.

6. Make as many connections as possible between your character and your readers. Even morally questionable characters eat, drink, breathe and enjoy the sunshine the same as everyone else. The more they do this, the more chance your readers have of making that connection.

7. Bad people have feelings, too. Make sure you always give them something – or someone – to love. Anyone can have that. Anyone who doesn't will never be a fully rounded character.

8. Don't distance yourself from your characters. Think about what would drive *you* to do the things your flawed or ambiguous characters do. And if you can't imagine it, then it probably won't be convincing enough for the reader to imagine, either.

9. Overcoming a personal flaw (e.g. cowardice, pride, the inability to love) can be an important part of the character's journey. If you're struggling to give your character an arc, that's a pretty good place to start.

10. Flaws are best shown in two ways: behaviour and interactions with other people. This is definitely the time to *show* your character's flaws in action.

5

Children

Because we've all been children, many writers assume that writing about childhood is easy. It isn't. Many authors struggle with depictions of children, simply because so many depictions of childhood in fiction are unrealistic, or cutesy, or sentimental, or – at the opposite end of the scale – sinister or creepy. Either way is likely to make your character flat and stereotypical.

1. Adults remember childhood through the lens of experience. Sometimes that works well in a narrative. But when you're trying to depict real children in the moment, the adult in you can get in the way. As adults, we have to understand that our memory is selective, and that what we *think* we remember isn't the complete picture.

2. We tend to forget a lot of things about ourselves in childhood. That's because experience teaches us to see life in a different way. To depict realistic child characters, we need to remember what it was like *not* to know the things we take for granted.

3. There is no such thing as a typical child, any more than there is 'typical' adult. Children are people. Everything you know about people – diversity of race, class, culture, ability, personality type, body shape, etc. – also applies equally here.

4. Children are often driven by motives that adults find illogical. That's because child logic is fundamentally different to adult logic. Adults are usually led by what they *know* of the world; but children, knowing less, are more likely to work on what they *believe.*

5. Children often exhibit imaginative behaviour patterns that, in an adult, might be construed as a sign of a mental-health issue. Seeing fairies in your garden, talking to invisible friends, seeking comfort via elaborate rules and rituals that adults don't always understand – all this can be perfectly standard child behaviour.

6. Adults often project on to children the thoughts and feelings they'd *like* them to have. But the human brain is not fully formed until the age of twenty or so: that means children and adolescents are sometimes perceived as cruel, self-centred, or lacking in empathy. They're not; but they do tend to have a different perspective to adults.

7. Children, like animals, can come across as cute, innocent or uncomplicated. In fact, like animals, they are complex beings, existing in a world of their own, often unaware of the stresses and crises in the lives of the adults around them.

8. When writing about children or teenagers, try to avoid using a lot of slang. Teen slang changes all the time. It will always be out of date by the time your book comes out.

9. Don't underestimate what children feel. Feelings are no less powerful or valid in a young person as with an older one. And many children – even the very young – are profoundly aware of death, and sex – as well as all the other things you think you're keeping from them.

10. Ideally, you should do your research by observing and talking to children. Your own, if you have them; or your young relatives or their friends. If that isn't possible, you might try going into schools, or reading books on child psychology, or watching documentaries on child behaviour. Children are no easier to write than adults; and if you want them to play a meaningful role in your fiction, you need to research them properly.

6

Relationships

Characters are often best viewed in terms of their relationships. The more relationships a character has, the more chance you have of portraying them in different roles – as a lover, a friend, an adversary, a sibling, a partner, a rival, a spouse. A character with no relationships stands very little chance of being convincing. So, as you're building a character, it's worth considering all the relationships they've had in their life; what makes them different, what patterns are repeated, and what all this tells you about the character you're exploring.

1. Sexual relationships can be very revealing. Intimacy – or the lack of it – can often lie at the heart of a character. What does intimacy reveal about the way your protagonist behaves? Does it make them trusting? Suspicious? Afraid? Anxious? Careless? And why?

2. Our relationship with our parents is often at the heart of our dealings with other people. There's a reason psychoanalysts nearly always want to hear about a patient's childhood. Go into your protagonist's past. What kind of parents did they have? Was your protagonist fractious? Obedient? Starved of love? Surrounded by warmth? Co-dependent? A carer? If their parents are still around, what is their relation-ship now? Is it the same as it used to be, or is it the complete opposite?

3. Friends are often key to understanding a character. Giving a cool and ambivalent character a warm and gener-ous friend (think Mr Darcy and Mr Bingley in *Pride and Prejudice*) can allow you, the writer, to hint at a hidden, softer side to them. And of course, a friend can give the protagonist someone to confide in, allowing the author to unpack some of their inner conflict.

4. Enemies and rivals are a means of showing your protago-nist in a situation of stress, adversity, fear. How do they cope with a challenge? Are they aggressive? Resentful? Cunning? Combative? Do they shy away from conflict? Do they meet a challenge head-on?

5. Children can be a means of seeing your protagonist's tender side – or alternatively, their own childhood damage. Seeing how your protagonist relates to children – their own, or the children of others – can provide another important piece in the puzzle.

6. Professional partners are often a staple of the detective and mystery genre. Having a partner to bounce ideas off makes it easier to explore the possibilities of a mystery or puzzle (think Mulder and Scully in *The X-Files*), and takes what is essentially a rather solitary conflict (*the detective vs. the mysterious opponent*) into a more sociable sphere. It's also quite a good way of establishing a contrast between the protagonist at home and the protagonist in a work environment.

7. It can be useful to think about the idea of **power and your protagonist**. What are they like when they are in a position of power over others? What are they like when they are faced with someone in authority? Do they fall in line? Do they change their accent, their mannerisms? Do they stand up straighter? Or do they stay exactly the same?

8. **The way you handle dialogue can be helpful in exploring some of these questions**. How does your protagonist communicate with the people in their life? Are they open and talkative? Monosyllabic? Profane? Do they deflect from emotional situations using humour?

9. **Do they have siblings?** If so, how do they behave when their siblings are around? Are they close? Always quarrelling? Still re-enacting events from the past?

10. **What or who makes them laugh?** Are they quick to laughter? Do they only let their defences down around certain people? Does their sense of humour run to the absurd? The macabre? Or do they not have much of a sense of humour at all?

7

Describing Characters

A lot of writers over-describe their characters, or concentrate on the wrong things. No one really needs a whole paragraph of description to create a mental picture: I think you can draw a thumbnail sketch in just a sentence or two, as long as you decide what to concentrate on.

1. In real life, we notice different things about people in different circumstances. Try keeping a little notebook, in which you write down your visual first impressions of people you see on the bus, in the café, in the street. Note the things you notice first.

2. Your readers don't need too many details. Find one initial, graphic image or detail to describe the character you're presenting, so that they can remember them. Too much will confuse and slow down the narrative.

3. If you're a white writer introducing a BAME character, you need to make their ethnicity clear from the start. Otherwise, your readers are likely to make the assumption that your character is white. In the same way, your audience is likely to assume that a character is cisgendered, neurotypical and physically abled unless you make it clear that they're not.

4. Don't forget, you can drip-feed information to your reader throughout the story – especially if this is information about a main character, who needs more detailing than the secondary characters.

5. Visual description is a useful way of delivering other character information, too. Think like a detective. Consider what you can convey about the individual's personality from their physical characteristics.

6. Try to think outside the box. Yes, there are obvious details you need to show your readers, but try to add things they wouldn't necessarily have thought of looking for, too.

E.g.: In *Madame Bovary*, Flaubert stresses two details about his protagonist: her sleek bands of dark hair, and her long hands, '*slightly dry at the fingertips*'. He paints an impressionistic overall picture, with the hint of a tactile detail, as well.

7. Don't forget non-visual indicators, too. Tone of voice, movement, speed or slowness of gestures, tension in posture, even scent. All these can be powerful tools in your descriptive arsenal.

8. Clothes and hairstyles can be a useful descriptor, but don't overuse them. Too often, eccentric clothing or hair can become a substitute for personality.

9. A graphic, self-contained image, especially in a comic context, can sum up a character perfectly. For example, from P.G. Wodehouse: '*He was a tubby little chap who looked as if he had been poured into his clothes and had forgotten to say "When!"*'

10. And don't forget that when writing from the perspective of a character, physical description can become a way of finding out how *they* see other people: the things they notice first; the interpretations they put on appearance. Imagine a character meeting your heroine for the first time. Think of the different effects of having them first notice: her luminous eyes, or her high-heeled shoes, or her strong voice, or her restless energy, or her scent, or the freckles on her collarbone.

8

Choosing Names

Choosing names for your characters is not just a matter of picking a name you *like*: it has to match the character you're writing, or it won't feel believable. That means really thinking about your character's background and origins.

1. Think of who chose the name, and why. Who were your character's parents? What names were popular in their day? Did they choose the name to honour someone in their family? Was there another reason?

2. Consider your character's background and class. Names often tend to reflect awareness of popular culture. Were your protagonist's parents likely to name them after someone in a book? A politician? A TV character? A rock star? A footballer? An actor?

3. Where in the country do your character's parents originate from? Some surnames are more likely to occur in certain regions of the country. It's worth checking the origin of your chosen name, to make sure it's properly authentic.

4. Is the character you're naming from another country? If so, all these considerations apply, and more. Take advice when you need to. It's all too easy to mess up by using an out-dated, inappropriate, or geographically or culturally unlikely name.

5. How old is your character? Names come in and out of favour all the time. This doesn't mean you can't give an old-fashioned or unusual name to a young character, but you'll have to give a reason for it. (For example: *'Young Elsie was named after her great-grandmother.'*)

6. Remember that your character will be using their name throughout their life. Choosing a name that only sounds appropriate to a young person in a romance (even if that's what you're writing) can be jarring when you imagine them older.

7. It's also important to distinguish between *what happens in life* and what *readers of fiction* will accept. 'Tiffany' is a perfectly historically appropriate name for an 18th-century heroine, but it sounds so contemporary that most readers just wouldn't believe in it. Similarly, it's perfectly possible for a real-life, present-day person to be called 'Atom', or 'Facebook', or 'Wildheart', but try it in fiction, and you may find that readers don't buy it, and that will alienate them from your story.

8. Just inventing names from scratch, even in a fantasy novel, isn't as straightforward as it sounds. All names have a provenance, a social and racial significance. And 'invented' names, even in fantasy, can sometimes be quite problematic when you unpick them. It's all too easy to unconsciously reflect a racial or cultural stereotype via a thoughtless choice of name.

9. Never just invent a 'foreign-sounding name' for a character of another ethnicity. J.K. Rowling's Cho Chang may *sound* Chinese to anyone who doesn't know a lot of Chinese names, but to someone who does, it might sound inauthentic and jarring.

10. Try to avoid, if you can, character names beginning with the same first letter, or that closely resemble each other, e.g. Mickey and Nicky, or Barry and Gary, or Caroline and Catherine. It makes it harder for readers (and editors) to tell one from another.

9

Women

Hang on a minute, I hear you say. *Isn't this a bit sexist?* Well, yes: the literary world *is* a bit sexist. Books with male protagonists are still regarded differently to books with women protagonists – and are much more likely to win prizes – and men and women are often still represented quite differently in fiction. That's why I think it's worth taking a look at the portrayal of women in particular, with a view to redressing the balance.

Historically, women protagonists have been largely limited to two literary spheres: the domestic and the romantic. And although some progress has been made, books by women (or featuring women protagonists) are still all too often viewed as 'women's interest', while books by men and about men are deemed universal and important. Perhaps that is why so many men have asked me for advice on writing convincing women characters. And although unconscious gender bias is not solely a male prerogative, men are still often more likely to write generic, flat female characters. Either way, if you think your women characters may be in need of defining, here are a few things to think about.

1. Women are allowed to drive. That means they can drive your story. They don't have to be anyone's wife, daughter, sacrifice, trusty sidekick, or love interest.

2. Women protagonists don't have to be young and conventionally attractive. Physical attractiveness is not the only way to make a female character interesting – in fact, arguably, it's probably the *least* interesting way to depict her, because it tells you nothing at all about her as a person.

3. We hear a lot from the industry about the need for 'strong women characters'. This has led to a large number of novels featuring sword-wielding, kick-ass heroines. And while this is perfectly okay, it's worth noting that your characters – whatever their gender – don't need to be aggressive, combative or trained in martial arts to be strong. Strength can be a human quality, as well as an indicator of muscle.

4. While love stories can be terrific, women's stories don't all have to be about the search for love. A woman's story is just as likely to be driven by something else – a cause, a friendship, a quest for self-knowledge, a conflict, a mystery, overcoming a personal flaw, the desire for revenge – as it is about finding love.

5. There are no exclusively 'feminine' characteristics. Women protagonists can be as ruthless, amoral, scheming or hateful as any of their male counterparts. In the same way, referring to a woman character as 'unusual' because she does everyday things like changing a car tyre, riding a motorbike or not caring much about her appearance isn't as progressive as some authors think it is.

6. Women characters in historical fiction (or historically inspired fantasy) are often confined by the author to the drawing room or the bedchamber. But women characters can exist in pretty much any setting, at any time in history. Be imaginative, and do your research. Your characters – and your readers – deserve more.

7. Even in the cases of acclaimed literary novelists like Jonathan Franzen, Michel Houellebecq or Haruki Murakami, **women characters are often portrayed almost exclusively in terms of their physicality.** That often leads to the creation of women characters whose identity is defined by pregnancy, sexual activity, physical attractiveness, or how often they (or the male protagonist) think about their breasts. (Top tip: *real* women very rarely think about their breasts at all – and certainly never in the way in which some male writers think they do.)

8. **Women in stories should not exist solely to give the male protagonist a reason to do things.** They can (and should) have their own agency, their own reasons to exist and participate in the journey. Too many women in fiction are used as a sacrifice to the plot, as in the ever-popular 'man-has-to-avenge-his-murdered-wife' scenario (*Mad Max, The Fugitive, Braveheart*), or the 'attractive young woman as murder victim' still too common in the detective genre. It's getting boring. Don't be that.

9. **Don't sexualize your female protagonist unless you're writing a sex scene.** As soon as you do that, the character loses any chance of becoming three-dimensional. Plus it's awkward for the reader, and takes them out of the story, as well as revealing more about the author than they might realize.

10. We all have unconscious gender bias. If you're having difficulty getting away from gender clichés and tropes, try first writing your protagonist as male, then gender-flipping them. It can make for some fresh and new discoveries (Ripley in the *Alien* movies, for example, was originally written as a male character).

10

Diversity

We hear a lot about the need for diversity in fiction. Mostly it's because there isn't enough of it in what is still currently – at least in the English-speaking world – a predominantly white, male-dominated, heterosexual, middle-class industry. That doesn't mean that anyone is trying to dictate to authors what to write, but for anyone looking for more interesting and authentic characters, it's useful to consider that our world is made up of much more than one type of person.

1. Diversity is not about 'being PC'. It's about making your characters more relevant and more believable. People in the real world come in all kinds of different packages. People in fiction should do the same.

2. Diversity isn't just about race. It's about gender, culture, body type, sexuality, age, social class, and physical and mental ability. Or indeed, any combination of these. Just like in the real world.

3. It's not a free pass for authors to use stereotypes. Diverse characters come in as many varieties as there are people in the world, and yours should do the same. Bear in mind that, for example, a Muslim character will have as much or as little chance of being like any other Muslim in the world as any random Christian, Jew, or atheist, etc. Class differences, racial differences, geographical location, educational background, language, economic group – all these things will mean tremendous differences in personality. So don't make assumptions about your characters. Get to know them properly.

4. Don't use your diverse characters uniquely as representatives of their cultural or racial group. No one speaks for the collective. You wouldn't assume a white accountant from Argyll to have the same views on race (for example) as a white maths teacher from New York, or a white window cleaner from Finland, or a white artist from Moscow.

5. Diversity is natural. There has never been a time in history, or a place on Earth, where it wasn't. That's why fantasy epics based on a 'European mediaeval' version of gender and race simply don't ring true. Even in mediaeval times, it's clear from the art and literature of the period that there was plenty of ethnic and cultural diversity in Europe, and plenty of examples of women in positions of social and political power.

6. No author need be afraid of imagining characters from groups they don't belong to. That's not appropriation. It's being a citizen of the world. Appropriation is trying to claim for yourself, or to reinvent, reduce or redefine someone else's unique culture or experience. Don't do that.

7. We do, however, have a responsibility to represent other people as honestly and as well as we can. **That means trying**

as far as possible to remove the distorting lenses of bias, assumption and stereotype. That isn't easy. First you need to accept that you may have bias in the first place. (Top tip: You do. We *all* do. The trick is overcoming it.)

8. It's easy for well-meaning people wishing to write more diverse characters to be culturally insensitive. Avoid this by consulting people who know more than you do. And, no – talking to just *one* person isn't enough. Just because your disabled friend thinks your blind character sounds authentic doesn't automatically mean they are. There is no 'typical' member of any one community. One person doesn't speak for a group. If you find that your character exists solely to represent a culture, viewpoint or condition, you didn't write a diverse character. You wrote a stereotype.

9. Anyone can be a hero. Diversity isn't just for sidekicks.

10. It's much easier to *write* diversely when you also *read* diversely and interact with lots of different people. Listen to other voices. Read books by diverse authors. Use sensitivity readers if you need them (and yes, you probably do). The more you do this, the more naturally you'll be able to take to diverse characterization.

PART 5

Detailing

This is where you look at the things that make your fictional world more real: sense-impressions, the weather, food; sensations, laughter – the thousand little details that make the difference between a scene that stays flat on the page and one that pulls the reader in.

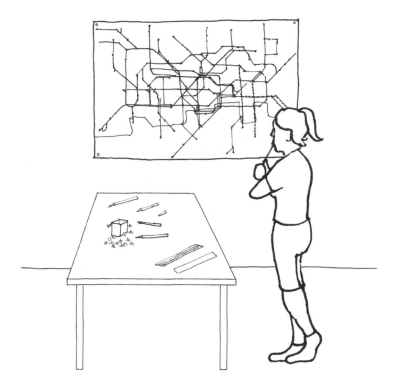

Now that she'd drawn it out there was
something about the plot structure of
Megan's novel about London Underground
train drivers that seemed oddly familiar.

1

The Weather

The weather is all around us. It affects every aspect of our lives. It changes our moods, it determines what we wear, we talk about it all the time – and yet it's often written badly, or left out altogether. But could *Wuthering Heights* have had the same impact without those depictions of wind-blasted moors? Or Dickens, with his soot-filled skies? Or J.G. Ballard's apocalyptic floods?

1. A lot of writers describe the weather when they can't think of anything else to describe, which is as dull and uninteresting as it sounds. Don't do this. Readers instinctively know to skip anything that feels like padding.

2. It's also an easy way to slip into cliché. (*Way* too many dark and stormy nights in literature.) Clichés mostly happen when people don't really think about what they're saying. Think harder. If *you're* not thinking deeply about what's happening in your story, neither will your readers.

3. If you mention the weather, then let it be for a reason. You could use it to create atmosphere, or to highlight its physical or psychological effect on your protagonist. (In Albert Camus' *The Outsider*, the protagonist shoots a man while under the influence of the midday heat and the sun's reflection on the water – it's arguably the driving force of the story.)

4. Don't comment on the obvious. We all know the rain's wet. But what does it sound like? Smell like? *Feel* like?

5. In some fiction the weather is often used to reflect a character's feelings (we call this the 'pathetic fallacy'). Nowadays, this can sometimes seem a little obvious or predictable, but it can be subverted to good effect.

6. The weather can affect your plot in all kinds of ways, from the gale that prevents you from leaving the house, to the tree branch tapping at the window, to the set of mysterious footsteps in the snow. In Donna Tartt's *The Secret History*, an unexpected fall of snow changes the whole course of the novel, creating an increasing tension around the search for a body that has an effect on every character in the book.

7. Be consistent. If you've established that it's raining, make sure your story reflects it. From time to time, remind your readers (the sound of the rain, the puddles, a car sending up a sheet of water as it drives by) to maintain the atmosphere.

8. The weather can be central to your characters' relationship with their environment. Compare the importance of weather to a homeless person, a professional driver, a teacher, a surfer, a shepherd. (In *Something Wicked This Way Comes*, Ray Bradbury uses deliberately naïve language to reflect the wonder felt by his child protagonist: 'The sun rose yellow as a lemon. The sky was round and blue. The birds looped clear water songs in the air.')

9. Remember to use all your senses. Imagine describing (for instance) rain in terms of sound, texture, temperature, light and scent. (Have a look at the following, from Angela Carter's *Burning Your Boats*: '*The lucidity, the clarity of light that afternoon was sufficient to itself; perfect transparency must be impenetrable, these vertical bars of brass-coloured distillation of light coming down from sulphur-yellow interstices in a sky hunkered with grey clouds that bulge with more rain. It struck the wood with nicotine-stained fingers, the leaves glittered. A cold day of late October, when the withered blackberries dangled like their own dour spooks on the discoloured brambles.*')

10. Weather can be a really good way of establishing a sense of place, but make sure to check your weather facts. Many a decent book has been ruined by the author forgetting that the climate of the place they're describing isn't that of their hometown.

2

The Seasons

Most writers spend a long time world-building and establishing a sense of place. But to really evoke a sense of *where*, you also need to bear in mind *when* your story is unfolding.

1. Seasonal changes may affect your story in different ways, depending on where it is set. If it's set in a rural location, seasonal changes may be more obvious than in an urban setting.

2. However, even in an urban location, changes in weather, light, temperature, climate and vegetation are likely to affect your surroundings (and therefore, your plot).

3. And in a more rural setting, it's vital to fact-check the details. You don't want your heroine going off to pick blackberries if they're four months out of season.

4. Are there leaves on the ground? Is there snow? Is the sun warm enough for Miss Bennett to take off her shawl? Is there ice on the road? Is it unseasonably hot? All these things are essential in building up a realistic atmosphere.

5. Then there are the other ways by which we define the turn of the year: holidays – Christmas, Easter, Hallowe'en, Ramadan, Eid, whatever occasions you may celebrate – or be aware of others celebrating.

6. These things affect cities, too: you may not notice the wildlife as much in an urban thriller, but you'd certainly expect to see Christmas lights, shop displays, bigger crowds, etc. in December.

7. Such details are part of the canvas of your story's setting, and as such, demand authenticity (and therefore, extra research). And remember, even if you've visited the place you're describing, Moscow in January isn't at all the same as Moscow in July.

8. Consider, among other things: the weather, cultural markers, changes in the natural world, the light (it's worth checking sunrise and sunset times), bank holidays, even moon phases, if you're writing about a verifiable time.

9. You don't have to mention *all* these things, but do keep them in mind; otherwise you may find yourself forgetting something important. There's a lot of useful info online, including archived calendars, almanacs, TV listings.

10. How do the seasons affect your protagonist? Does it change their behaviour? Their mood? Are they depressed in winter? All these things can, and should, be linked into your narrative. Remember, nothing in your story should exist in isolation.

3

Scents

Scent is often a neglected area in writing fiction. And yet it is possibly the most evocative and intuitive of the senses. There are many ways to use it in fiction – to create atmosphere, to add realism, to give an extra dimension to a character.

1. Scent – and what it conjures up – can reveal a lot about a person. Some actors like to allocate scents to their protagonists in order to get into character: writers, too, can do the same thing. It doesn't have to be perfume; it could be the scent of diesel oil, or burnt toast, or roses. Either way, you can use it to unlock a part of your protagonist's personality and to make a connection.

2. Scents can introduce surprising, new elements into scenes. For example, most people can imagine how a battle *sounds*, but not necessarily how it *smells*.

3. Scent can evoke memories, too, giving you insights into your protagonist's character, their past and their emotions.

4. Some scents are part of the collective consciousness: cut grass, your grandmother's house, Bonfire Night, a spring day at school. Use them to make connections with your readers.

5. Scent is a great way to create intimacy, giving a different dimension to scenes of tenderness between characters.

6. It's not always easy to describe a scent, except in terms of other scents, sensations or memories. One way is just to list the things the scent contains (for example: *'The room smelt of sweat, and cigar smoke'*). This works well in small doses, but you might need to vary it, too.

7. Another way is to link the scent to other sensations. (For example: *'The sharp, hot reek of the lion's cage.'*) In this case it's easier to communicate the scent via other, perhaps more direct sensations.

8. The final way is via scent association, or what the scent evokes. (E.g. *'She smelt of home, and summertime, and evenings by the fireside.'*) This is a more abstract way of conveying scent, but it goes straight to the emotions.

9. Try rewriting a scene in your story, replacing every visual image by a scent-impression. See how this changes the mood of the scene.

10. Learn to improve your scent memory: close your eyes and determine what a familiar place smells like. Try it on the bus, in your house, outside. Write down your findings.

4

Colours

Because most people have a visual imagination, colour is often the easiest and most graphic way for an author to describe something. However, if that's your go-to method of bringing a scene to life, it can get samey very fast, as well as effectively excluding the 25 per cent or so of readers who don't have a visual imagination. Here are a few ideas on how to expand your colour palette.

1. Put down the thesaurus. Some people try to create variety by using more unusual colour vocabulary (cerulean, viridian, madder, etc.). But if you use terms that your readers don't recognize, you lose the visual impact of using colour imagery at all. Varying your vocabulary is fine, of course, but unless your reader already *knows* that 'cerulean' is a shade of blue, they'll either not know what you're describing at all, or they'll have to interrupt their reading to look up the word. Either way, you've lost them.

2. Think about the *feel* and *textures* of colours. Think about the difference between *cool* blue and *warm* blue; *hot* pink and *dusty* pink; *fresh* green and *dull* green. None of these sensations are really directly related to colour, and yet we know exactly what they mean.

3. Or you can link your chosen colour to something your readers will find easier to visualize. Think of the variations between 'ice blue', or 'forget-me-not blue', or 'electric blue', or 'sky blue'.

4. Some comparisons are so very common that they descend into cliché. Try to avoid things like 'blood red', 'jet black' or anything else that seems so obvious that you might as well not say it at all.

5. You can create some interesting effects by making a more personal comparison. For example: *Her dress was precisely the same colour as the green triangle in a box of Quality Streets.* This kind of use of colour reveals more about the narrator, giving insights about what they notice and what associations the colour has for them.

6. As with all description, avoid focusing on the obvious. Unless you tell them otherwise, your readers will probably assume the sky is blue anyway. So if you want to make them sit up, tell them something they don't know.

7. Bear in mind that not everyone experiences colour in the same way. For that reason, you can use it as part of your characterization. How do your characters process colour? What memories and associations do colours hold for them?

8. We often associate colours with feelings. That's why we sometimes *feel blue; see red;* have *dark moods.* As a writer, you're in control of your world, and you can use your colour palette as a more or less subtle means of hinting at your chosen character's state of mind.

9. There are only so many colours a reader can visualize at once. Unless you're intending to cause mental chaos in your readers, it's a good idea to limit the colour theme to one or two colours at a time.

10. Writing colours is a bit like highlighting a piece of text. Don't feel the need to tell the reader *everything*, but if a detail is likely to be important later in your narrative, assigning a colour to it (e.g. *The girl in the red coat, the pink-painted house, the black car*) is a good way to keep it in the reader's mind.

5

Food

There is a long, long tradition of using food in fiction, dating back many centuries. That's because food is one of the few completely universal human experiences. Everyone *understands* food: the process of cooking, nostalgic food, cravings, food for pleasure, hunger, deprivation, food as a celebration, sharing food with family, even food as guilt. As such, it's an excellent chance to engage directly with your readers.

1. Fairytales are filled with food. From Aphrodite's golden apple to the Hogwarts feasts, it has often been linked with magic. No surprise there: magic and food are both about transformation. And when you're writing fantasy, it's important to ground it in reality where you can: it makes the fantasy aspects of your story easier to relate to.

2. Food is also often linked with memory, nostalgia, family and culture. It's a powerful way of looking into the past and the origins of a character; of understanding where they have come from.

3. Writing about food is often coded sensuality: a well-written food scene can sometimes be more sensual and evocative than an actual sex scene.

4. Food is a great tool for revealing aspects of a character's personality. Do they love food? Do they feel anxious around it? Are they social eaters? Do they enjoy preparing meals for others? Do they simply use food as fuel, or is it important to them in other ways?

5. Food can be a good starting point when establishing a sense of place. It's a kind of universal language that brings people together. What kind of food is typical? How does it reflect the nature of those who live there? What are their food customs?

6. Food is multisensory. When describing it, remember you can use scent, texture, colour, even sound, as well as taste.

7. Meals are a great opportunity to bring characters together. You can use them to show how your characters interact with others – or not – in social situations.

8. It's also a good way of marking important points in your plot. Big arrivals and departures are often celebrated in fiction by feasts; as well as victories, coronations, and moments of calm and relief after long periods of tension.

9. Food is more often about feelings than about the physical act of eating. Describing the act of chewing and swallowing is usually less interesting and appealing than describing the feelings, memories and thoughts that the food evokes.

10. Food can be delicious, but it isn't always a positive. It can also be a way of exploring ideas like deprivation, self-denial, poverty, disgust, guilt, eating disorders and the conflicted, anxious feelings about food that many people – especially Westerners – can experience. For example, Margaret Atwood's *The Edible Woman* explores this sense of existential disconnection from food and physicality.

6

Sex

Sex is another of those universal human experiences that can help build a connection between your readers and your characters. It's hard to write a good love story without some kind of physical intimacy, and yet, many otherwise excellent writers write sex so badly that there's even an award for it – the largely male-dominated Bad Sex Award – for the worst offenders. Here's how to avoid ever being nominated.

1. People talk about 'sex scenes' as if they were separate from the rest of the story. They shouldn't be. Like any other scene, a scene of physical intimacy should have a purpose, a meaning, an arc. No one needs to add sex into a book to 'make it interesting'. Gratuitous sex is no better than any other form of padding.

2. A sex scene should teach you something about your characters. What are they like in an intimate situation? How do they feel about each other? How do they express their physicality? Their vulnerability? What do they think about? If it doesn't deliver something new, consider whether you need it at all.

3. Sex should never be thoughtless or formulaic. Not all sex feels the same every time, even with the same partner.

4. Not all real-life sex is good sex. Nor does it have to be in fiction. Awkward, unsuccessful, unsatisfying sex can be more revealing than the generic, performative kind.

5. Sex covers a lot more than just intercourse. The most erotic scenes in literature are often the least explicit.

6. Sex isn't something one person does *to* another. Make sure both partners get to participate.

7. As a rule, anatomy is boring. As with food scenes, a sex scene is a lot less about the physical act, and more about feelings, sensations and reactions.

8. Sex doesn't always have to be between a young, able-bodied, conventionally attractive heterosexual couple. In fiction, it often is; but if you want your fiction to come to life, remember that diversity exists everywhere, even in the bedroom.

9. This isn't about you. You're not writing this scene to turn yourself on, or to convince the world you're a sex god (it won't), but to serve your story and to learn more about your characters.

10. This isn't the time to go for really complicated imagery. Sex, like food, is down to earth, and piling on the similes and metaphors usually ends up sounding ludicrous.

7

Pain

Physical sensations are often notoriously tricky to describe, except in terms of other sensations. That's why the language of physical pain – like the language of sex – is so often riddled with clichés and hyperbole.

1. Lots of writers just fall back on things like: 'the pain was indescribable', which frankly just sounds incompetent.

2. Others fall into the trap of overcomplicating their imagery, therefore reducing its impact. Ideally, you need something graphic and simple that doesn't affect the flow of your narrative.

3. As with a good sex scene, less is more. Leave something for the imagination.

4. It also needs to be something your readers can relate to. Most people know what a cut or a burn feels like: the trick is to get them to imagine something they've experienced, but worse.

5. If you can, channel your own experience. We tend not to remember pain when it's gone, so try to jot down your feelings and sensations as you encounter them, for later use in your writing.

6. Make sure you get the physical details right. Research them if you need to. There's nothing worse than getting biological facts wrong for pulling a reader out of the story.

7. **There are many, many kinds of pain**, from the sharp pain of a fresh injury to the relentless throb of a headache. You have plenty of sensations to choose from, and therefore no excuse to be unimaginative.

8. Pain isn't just about description. It's a great characterization tool – a way of showing what your characters are really like under different kinds of pressure. Are they stoic? Patient? Do they lash out? Lie about their feelings?

9. Mental pain can be as acute, as diverse, as relatable to and as revealing as physical pain. Don't forget to use it, too.

10. Bear in mind that **the better your description of physical sensation or emotional turmoil, the more likely your readers are to empathize**. Some may even be upset by it. That's no reason for you to change what you write, but sometimes a warning – perhaps in the jacket copy – can help if you're dealing with a potentially gruelling subject.

8

Action

Action scenes include fight scenes, chase scenes, physical confrontations – any scene in which action takes precedence over dialogue, atmosphere or characterization. That doesn't mean those things can't also be present, but they tend to be handled differently.

1. A good action scene stays in the mind's eye. Make it graphic and visual.

2. Don't neglect physical sensations – scent, sound, touch, pain. Just don't linger on them for too long.

3. Keep imagery sparse and well-chosen: you won't have much time to make poetic comparisons during a fight or a chase scene. **But a single well-placed detail** – a torn fingernail, the sound of birds singing, a piece of litter blown by the wind – can carry heightened impact.

4. Remember that in moments of stress and heightened adrenalin, you don't experience things in the same way as you would in a relaxed situation. Time works differently – sometimes seeming to move faster, sometimes more slowly – than usual.

5. In situations of stress, we notice things differently. We focus on some details and not on others (even obvious ones). It's not unusual to have disconnected, even inappropriate thoughts.

6. In real life, fights are usually over in a matter of seconds. And in a fight situation, most people aren't thinking all that clearly about what they're doing with their body. Even if your protagonist is a specialist in martial arts, they are more likely to rely on muscle memory than be thinking clearly about whether a specific blow is a left hook or an uppercut.

7. If you're writing physical detail, aim to make it authentic. A lot of otherwise good writing is let down by the author's suggestion that a bullet wound can heal in twenty-four hours. The same goes for weapon detail. Only remember to ask yourself whether your *protagonist* knows (or cares) that the handgun is a Glock 9mm semi-automatic, or whether *you're* the one who needs to know.

8. Action doesn't necessarily mean the same as violence. Nor does a scene need to be violent to be dramatic, powerful or emotionally charged.

9. By all means portray violence, but try not to perpetuate harmful tropes while you're doing it. Storylines that celebrate violence (or sexualize it, or link it with power and success, or portray it as the answer to problems) make it harder to combat the growth of those ideas in real life. In the same way, try not to make scapegoats out of marginalized groups. Too many people already automatically link racial characteristics, social class, or mental illness with violence. We can do better.

10. Think about what you're portraying, and why. This isn't to set limits to the level of violence you're choosing to portray (that's your business, and that of your story), but to be sure of what message you're aiming to convey. For instance, if you write about sexual violence as if it's an aberration, and have characters express loathing for the crime, you set a very different tone than if you portray it as some kind of natural imperative by an apex predator.

9

Feelings

One of the most challenging things about writing a story is how to make the reader *feel* what the author wants them to feel. Fear, sympathy, hunger, delight – all of these are possible, as long as you're able to channel your words into feelings. Sounds easy? It's not. It takes a bit of self-awareness to convey authentic feelings, and you're going to have to let go of your fear and make yourself vulnerable to the reader. That can be daunting. Keep at it: this is how you make that vital connection which makes your words cross continents, touch lives and make people smile.

1. There is no substitute for authenticity. If you want an authentic reaction, you need to be authentic yourself. That doesn't necessarily mean writing autobiographically (although that works too). But it does mean being emotionally honest and articulate. That isn't always easy.

2. Emotional articulacy takes practice. If you're afraid or reluctant to explore your feelings in real life, you may find it hard to do in your writing.

3. Some writers tend to use humour as a means of self-defence, of deflecting from their deeper feelings. But doing this is the equivalent of stepping away from an offered embrace. It distances you from the reader.

4. Know your limitations. If you've never actually experienced the feeling you're trying to describe (e.g. being a parent, being in love), you may not be able to write about it convincingly.

5. Do your research. Study other writers, especially those who write convincingly about deeply held beliefs and strong emotions. Consume evocative art of all kinds. Painting, music, theatre, dance – write down how it makes you feel and what it makes you remember.

6. Look into your own past. Seek out the events that made you feel most intensely. Write down what the memories evoke. This may not always be comfortable, so by all means set limits to what you're prepared to uncover – but know that the further you're willing to go, the further you'll take your readers.

7. Feelings often relate to sensual experiences. Use all your senses, both in examining your own deep feelings and in describing them.

8. Be honest. Readers will forgive you for making them cry as long as you're heartfelt and sincere. But trivializing their feelings, or faking yours, is the sign of a second-rate writer.

9. Be warned: on the way to achieving a greater level of emotional depth and articulacy, **you may tap into memories, feelings and experiences that upset or disturb you**. This is part of the process, but only you can decide how far to take it. And remember – *you*'re in control here. You make the decisions.

10. One of the consequences of making yourself vulnerable is that it will make you more likely to feel hurt or upset at any potential negative comments or reviews. I'm afraid there's no escaping this. But for every person who sneers at you, remember this: there may be someone else out there whose life you change for ever.

10

Humour

When writing comedy, it's helpful to remember that there's nothing inherently 'light' or simple about humour. It can centre on exactly the same themes as those you might find in tragedy, but it's usually much, much harder to write.

1. Humour can be an element in any kind of fiction. Comic relief can be very effective, even in the darkest and most challenging novels.

2. No theme is too dark for humour, but it's important to handle sensitive issues in the right way. Dark humour is not the same as cruelty, oppression or hate, and shouldn't be used to encourage those things.

3. Excellent characterization is at the heart of all really well-written humour, and when dealing with darker themes (depression, suicide, etc.) it's even more important for characters to be believable and well-drawn.

4. Keep asking yourself: 'Who are we laughing with, and who gave us permission?' Humour is about recognition and self-knowledge, not ridicule. So for instance, if your character has depression, make sure you're laughing with them, not at them.

5. Comedy is often about life experience, and what we learn from what we have undergone. Certain themes are very difficult to write about without having lived through that experience, and in comedy, are particularly hard to fake. This is a good time to write what you know.

6. Don't punch down. Unless you were the kind of kid who thought pulling the wings off flies was hilarious, it's not the way to get laughs.

7. Remember: you're not the one who gets to decide if something is funny. That's the audience's job. If the audience doesn't laugh, you didn't write a comedy.

8. Humour is both honest and humble. If you're afraid of laughing at yourself, don't attempt to write humour.

9. Humour – especially dark-themed humour – is open and self-aware. If you're uncomfortable exploring your feelings, you probably won't write good comedy.

10. Tutoring creative writing, I've met a lot of young writers who try to avoid writing about real emotions by hiding behind flippancy or shock tactics. This approach nearly always fails, though. **Comedy needs courage**.

PART 6

The First Draft

Hooray! You're nearing the end of your first draft. Chances are you're not satisfied with it yet – you may even think it's terrible. Full disclosure: *all first drafts are terrible.* You can expect to rewrite a novel multiple times before you're satisfied with the result. But it's much easier to rework a less-than-perfect draft than to try and perfect it as you go. Here are some suggestions on how to approach the next stage.

1

The First Draft

Your first draft is the first more or less complete version of your story. It may go through a number of changes before you decide it's finished, but once you have a rough first draft, you have something to build on. After that, it's a question of refining, restructuring, editing and checking, preferably with the help of a professional editor and copy-editor, before you're ready to submit it.

1. At this stage some writers like to create a detailed synopsis or diagram of their first draft, marking the important plot points, beats, reversals and surprises. This can help you understand whether your plot is the right overall shape.

2. Others would rather allow their story to develop organically, and work on the structure and pacing once the first draft is complete. That's fine, too; there's no single way to reach your goal (although if you like to let your book grow organically, you may have to do more pruning and weeding later on).

3. Just get on with it. It's tempting to tinker about with your first draft as you go along, but, barring a small amount of day-to-day line-work, which might help you get into the mood for writing, it's nearly always better to just get your draft down. Even a dirty first draft is easier to work with than a clean first chapter.

4. *All* **first drafts are more or less dirty**. That's fine: finessing the thing will come later.

5. **A first draft doesn't need to be written in any kind of order**. You may want to write the end first; or concentrate on key episodes as they occur to you. That's perfectly fine: lots of authors work this way, assembling the scenes in order once they have the essentials down.

6. **If you're on a roll writing a fast-paced sequence, you may find it helps to skip any slower, intervening scenes**. If so, put a place marker in your text (e.g. *Conversation between X and Y about Z*), to make sure you don't forget about it in your haste to push on.

7. **Writing a first draft takes time**. Depending on how fast you write and how much time you have available, it might be a year or longer before you have something usable.

8. **Don't be tempted to submit a first draft to potential agents** or publishers. If you work with an editor or beta reader, you might find it useful to enlist their help at this point, or you may prefer to wait until you have a cleaner draft before you choose to involve anyone else.

9. **Know what to look for in your first draft**. Think of it as a preliminary sketch of your finished work. Concentrate on getting the shape of the composition right first; you can have fun adding details and colours later.

10. Once you have a first draft, it's helpful to put it aside for a while (I like to leave it at least three months). You'll be able to return to it with a fresh eye and a better sense of what needs to be done to take it to the next level.

2

Rewriting

The process of writing is largely a process of *rewriting*. It's more than likely that, having come up with a rough first draft, you'll need to rewrite it several times before you achieve a satisfactory result. Don't rush this: it's essential. Give it all the time it needs.

1. Rewriting generally differs from close editing in that you're more likely to be looking at **structural redrafting, characterization and plotting** than matters of phrasing and style.

2. Give yourself plenty of space before you approach a rewrite. You need to give yourself enough objectivity to deal with what needs to be done properly.

3. First, read the whole thing through to make sure it reads smoothly. Is your story the right shape? Does it have a beginning, a development and a satisfactory ending? Does it feel too slow in parts, or does it feel rushed or jerky?

4. If you sense that there's a structural problem, it might help to go back to the basics of your structure. Plot it out as a graph, if it helps. Mark the moments of rising tension. See where the beats fall. Cut, expand or relocate as required.

5. How does it feel, coming back to your world? Do you get a gradual sense of discovery, or is there a big info-dump at the start? Do the details need filling in to make it seem more real to you? If it doesn't convince you, it won't convince the reader.

6. How does it feel coming back to your characters? Do you still believe in them, or are they unfinished and shadowy? Do you understand why they do what they do? If you don't, neither will anyone else.

7. Does the story start in the right place? Are you intrigued and engaged from the very beginning, or does it take too long to get going?

8. How's your narrative-to-dialogue ratio? Too much unbroken narrative can make for heavy reading. Too much dialogue can make it feel unfinished. Skim through your manuscript, and make sure there's a reasonable distribution of both.

9. Is your pay-off good enough? It's easy, in the early stages of drafting, to rush or mishandle the ending. Does it achieve what you wanted? Will it leave the reader satisfied?

10. Know that, however much you've already rewritten your manuscript, you're going to have to do it again at least once in response to queries from your editor. Don't rush the process. It takes time.

3

Troubleshooting

If, like me, you tend to allow your plot to evolve in a fluid way, rather than planning ahead, you're likely to find yourself having to deal with one or more of these problems when it comes to the editing stage . . .

1. The Bad Beginning. Ensure your readers are drawn into the story as early as you possibly can. Info-dumping, excessive scene-setting, or long inroads into character backstory can usually all be dispensed with until you've got your reader hooked.

2. The Saggy Middle. It's easy to build up tension at the beginning of a book, but round about the middle, there's often a moment when the plot sags. This is the time to look at your plot structure, to make sure there's still enough tension to keep it going, to identify where it starts to sag, and to rebuild it as necessary.

3. The Plot Bunny. Chasing a plot bunny or rogue subplot can sometimes lead you dangerously far from your main plot. If this happens, you'll need to be brutal. Go back to where you left your plot, and cut away the excess. And you never know, it may be useful later.

4. The Plot Hole. These tend to happen when you haven't thought out all the logistics of your developing plot. Maybe you've overlooked the timeline, or you've neglected a character. You're probably going to have to drop in a scene or two to fill in the gaps.

5. The Strangulena Effect. As demonstrated in Roger Zelazny's ambitiously complicated fantasy *Roadmarks*, this is where the author of a complex plot loses sight of a key player for long enough to forget about them altogether. And if you do, you might ask yourself whether you really needed them at all.

6. The Attack of the Killer Plot Device. This happens when a key element of your plot emerges too conveniently to be entirely plausible, thereby causing damage to your readers' suspension of disbelief. There's no escaping this one, I'm afraid. You're going to have to let it go. It may mean reworking some parts of your plot – but that's better than losing your readers' respect.

7. The Cup of Tea Syndrome. This is the classic rushed ending flaw: when you're so eager to get to the end of the story that you botch the ending. Give it three weeks, then write it again, making sure you give it time to reach its climax properly.

8. The Brick Wall. This is most common with writers like me, who don't always plan every aspect of the plot ahead: sometimes you just can't figure out where the plot will go to next. Don't beat yourself up: give it time. Work on something else for a bit, and the missing piece will come to you eventually.

9. The Underwhelming Plot Twist. This is where the plot builds up to something less than a climax. Maybe it's just not surprising enough. Maybe it's *too* surprising, because you haven't foreshadowed sufficiently. Either way, it's a deal breaker. You'll need to rethink it completely.

10. The About-Turn. This is where, having promised your readers one genre of book, you end up delivering another (a romantic novel that turns into a sci-fi halfway through, for instance). It can be done, but it rarely works. Most times, it's a plot-killer.

4

Directions

So what happens when you've lost the plot? Faced with a multiplicity of potential choices, it can be hard to keep track of where the journey is taking you. Here are a few ideas on what to do if you feel that your plot is unravelling:

1. The plot of your novel is a vehicle, driven by your protagonist, through the landscape of your imaginary world. Therefore, **first, know your protagonist**.

2. **Know also the relationship your protagonist has with their world**. Choose an adjective to describe each one. For example: a *good* person in a *bad* world, a *strong* person in a *hostile* world, a *timid* person in a *confusing* world, etc.

3. **Your protagonist's defining characteristic will determine how they drive** the plot vehicle across the terrain you give them. Are they reckless? Aggressive? Careful? These things will all affect their driving.

4. **It will also to some extent determine *where* they choose to go**. A writer who knows their characters should be able to predict the choices they are likely to make when faced with obstacles and challenges.

5. The type of terrain is determined by what kind of journey your characters are on. Is it a wild, exciting ride? A more sedate journey of self-discovery? A romantic drive into the sunset?

6. Once again, knowing your characters will help you determine how they will approach the journey. Eyes closed? Eagerly watching the road? Driving full-tilt at obstacles? Avoiding them entirely?

7. As a writer, you may feel that you are faced with a bewildering number of choices. But looking more closely at challenging situations from your character's unique perspective, you'll find the choices are much more limited.

8. If in doubt, you're probably complicating things too much. You might find it useful to try out your character in the context of a tabletop role-playing game like Dungeons & Dragons. Practise playing your character and making decisions on their behalf. See how those decisions shape the story.

9. Or step away from your book for a while and run a few challenging scenarios past your protagonist. How would they respond if they saw someone being mugged? If someone was mistreating an animal? If they witnessed an accident? If a relative died?

10. If you don't know the answer to these questions, then your character isn't yet qualified to drive the vehicle. Get to know them better before you put them in the driver's seat or, at the first sign of trouble, they're likely to crash your plot.

5

Editing

Editing is the stage that follows any rewriting or redrafting. You may have to go through several stages of editing before you finally get a finished draft. Your editor (if you have one) will make suggestions on how to approach the work, but it's your responsibility to implement their suggestions (or to think of better solutions to the problems they may have identified). If you don't yet have an editor, now's the time to think about finding one: self-editing is fine up to a certain point, after which you'll need a fresh pair of eyes to help you get to the next stage.

1. Editing is an essential and very personal part of your process. If you tend to over-write, it will involve *cutting* sections of overlong or unnecessary text. If you tend to write in less detail during the initial stages, then you'll probably need to *expand* your text during this stage.

2. Don't grieve over the text you cut. Think of it as the scaffolding you needed to use to build the house. Once the house is finished, you take the scaffolding away.

3. Read your text aloud. This will show you how well your story flows, whether certain passages are overlong or underwritten, whether your dialogue sounds natural or not. Don't worry if it seems odd to do this at first; you'll get used to it. And it is the best editorial tool you have.

4. Change the font you're using. It's a quick and easy way to look at your work with new eyes.

5. How can you tell if something needs cutting? If, when you're reading aloud, you find yourself wanting to skip ahead, then chances are the passage you've reached needs a trim. The same goes for over-long sections of dialogue that don't seem to lead anywhere, descriptions that don't add anything to what you've written previously, or scenes that don't contribute enough to the action of your story.

6. The editing stage is also the stage at which you find and weed out stylistic tics and over-repeated words or phrases. Everyone has these – identify yours, and be ruthless. Is your character nodding too often? Constantly flicking hair out of their eyes? Now's the time to stop them. Your manuscript will be better for it.

7. You'll probably find, too, that this is the time to **refine your dialogue**, and remove those pesky adverbs and dialogue tags.

8. If you're the kind of writer who likes to sketch out their first draft before filling in the fine detailing, you might find yourself *adding* material at this point. Things to consider at this stage might be: details of characterization, sense-impressions, feelings, atmosphere – those small but important touches that enable your reader to experience your story in as many different ways as possible.

9. This is the time to look back at your style. Is the language evocative? Are you using clichés? Would your work benefit from extra detail, or does your description need reining back?

10. Once you've finished an edit, **you may need to go back to your beta reader or editor**. Chances are they've already seen your first draft, and advised you accordingly. Now's the time to find out whether your redrafting really works, and how close you are to a finished manuscript. Don't be disheartened if you need to go through several rounds of redrafting and editing. Some authors edit over a dozen times before their work is publishable. It may seem frustrating, but it matters. You owe yourself – and your readers – the best possible end result.

6

Why Do I Need an Editor?

At first-draft stage, it's likely that you don't already have an editor. Perhaps you mean to self-publish, or to submit to an agent in order to get a traditional publishing deal.

Whatever your ambition, if you're planning to make your work public, you're going to need an editor or beta reader at some stage – preferably a professional with some knowledge of the business. Even if you're at the submitting-to-an-agent stage, having a properly edited and corrected manuscript can only work in your favour. Here are some of the reasons why *everyone* needs an editor:

1. Because no one, however talented, can be completely objective about their writing. And because no one, however meticulous, can spot *all* the mistakes in a text they've written themselves.

2. Because you owe it to your readers – and to yourself – to produce the best work you can, with as few mistakes as possible.

3. Because your editor will act as your first independent reader: they provide the dry run for your story before you send it out to an audience.

4. Because editors are avid and informed readers, with knowledge of the book industry. A good editor will know how to make your book more appealing to that audience you're hoping for.

5. Because if you don't have an editor to point out your mistakes, you can be sure the reviewers will do it – and a lot less tactfully.

6. Because anything your editor doesn't think is clear enough will probably confuse your readers, too.

7. Because having an editor is a valuable lesson in dealing with criticism. And if you listen to your editor, you won't have to deal with as much criticism from readers and reviewers.

8. Because even the most careful author has blind spots. And because anyone who thinks they don't need an editor is precisely the person who needs one most.

9. Because if you're aiming to submit work to an agent, you need your manuscript to stand out in a *good* way, and not because it's poorly finished.

10. Because it takes more than one person to make a book, and a good editor can be a collaborator, confidant and advisor on the journey to publication.

7

Refining Your Characters

Characterization is the process of bringing a fictional character to life. By now your characters should be fully rounded, with recognizable characteristics, a meaningful past, personal mannerisms, ambitions, feelings, flaws, fears, limitations – and everything else that makes up a human being. But are they *alive*? Here's a checklist.

1. Have you established sufficiently how your protagonist has been shaped by their past? Look for examples. You should have at least a couple.

2. Have you established how your protagonist has been shaped by their interactions with other characters? What experience have they gained? What lessons have they learnt?

3. By now you need to understand fully how your protagonist experiences the world. What kind of things do they notice first? What's their dominant sense? Are they able-bodied? Neurotypical? How does their physicality affect their mental processes?

4. How much has your protagonist changed throughout the story? Make list of what they were like at the beginning of your narrative, and the ways in which they've changed by the end of the story. If you can't think of anything meaningful, you may need to look at their arc again.

5. Look at your protagonist's dialogue. By now they should have an individual style. Do they talk a lot? Reveal a lot about their inner thoughts? Play down their feelings? Go quiet when they are upset?

6. With secondary characters, you need to check that they're interesting and colourful enough to come to life in your story. Now might be time to make them more distinct, more diverse, and to work on their individual style.

7. The best resource for refining characters I've come across is Konstantin Stanislavski's *An Actor Prepares*. Most of the techniques he recommends for actors getting into character work equally well for writers.

8. No named character should exist uniquely to serve the story. There should always be more to them than that. If not, now's the time to refine them.

9. No named character should exist uniquely to serve your protagonist. It helps if you can portray them at least once talking to another character on another subject.

10. Make sure you don't have too many secondary characters. If you're finding it hard to keep track, ask yourself what their role is. If they have exactly the same role as another character, consider whether you need them both. Or maybe you can combine them into one, more rounded character.

8

Believability

We've all been there: inserted a real-life detail into fiction, only to be told it isn't believable. Doesn't seem fair, does it? And yes, life is full of weirdness and randomness. But to be believable, even fiction has its *rules*. At this stage you need to be asking yourself: Is this story believable?

1. Yes, coincidences happen in life. But when they happen in fiction at just the right time to serve the plot, the reader starts to disconnect. *One* coincidence can work. More is a definite plot-killer.

2. There's a big difference between *realism* and *believability*. As an author, you can totally have one without the other. In *Harry Potter* we can easily accept characters riding in a flying car, because the rules of flying cars have already been established. On the other hand, readers might have had difficulty suspending their disbelief if Professor Snape had been revealed to have had a secret girlfriend, even though in real-world terms, that would be more *realistic*.

3. Realism is often limiting, dull and antagonistic to the process of storytelling. In life, things often happen for no reason, conflicts stay unresolved and nothing happens for long periods of time. Not so in fiction.

4. If someone criticizes your work as 'unrealistic', they're really saying it isn't *believable*. Your job is to make it so.

5. A storyteller's job is to make readers believe – or at least, suspend their disbelief – in all kinds of unrealistic, untested or unproven things. But just saying 'It's fiction' doesn't do that. Which is why coincidences are a weak plot device.

6. One of the best ways of achieving believability is giving the reader real emotional investment and insight into the characters. That's why, arguably, BoJack Horseman (a talking horse) is more *emotionally* believable than, for instance, James Bond. That's because we get to know in detail why BoJack makes the mistakes he does, where his character flaws come from, and why his self-destructive nature leads him into such repeatedly negative patterns of behaviour. In the case of Bond, we know next to nothing about his past, or his motivations, or his feelings. All we see is his behaviour in the moment.

7. Another is making sure that your world – however fantastic it is – is logically anchored according to its own set of rules. If your world is a magical world in which magic comes from spells in Latin, you won't be able to switch to a magical system based on runes or potions or dragons, without giving a very good reason.

8. It's helpful to include down-to-earth, relatable physical details in narratives to counterbalance any supernatural elements. Look how often Harry Potter characters eat, or how much sweating, belching and farting Stephen King characters do.

9. A good rule of thumb is to **include at least four realistic details for each of your unrealistic ones.** So Narnia – a magical kingdom, accessible through a wardrobe, where animals talk – is otherwise subject to the everyday rules of geography, the weather, social interactions, afternoon tea, etc.

10. Whatever you write, however convincing you are, there will always be some people who are not convinced. All you can do is try, and know that suspension of disbelief is voluntary, and that the reader's own beliefs may be beyond your control.

9

Foreshadowing

Unlike Life, which often throws stuff at you without any warning, a story needs to be constructed according to a very particular logic to be believable and satisfying to the reader. Foreshadowing is one of the ways we can make that happen.

1. Foreshadowing is the part of a story that ensures that nothing happens entirely at random, or without in some way preparing the reader for what's going to happen. Basically, it's a more subtle version of the ominous music in the soundtrack of a horror movie that gives us a hint of *something* about to happen.

2. To preserve the element of surprise, that hint can be *very* subtle; but once the reader has reached the payoff, they should be able to think back to the moment at which the clue was delivered, and go *'Aha! That all makes sense now!'*

3. Chekhov once expressed it as the concept of a gun, which, once introduced into the narrative, must at some point be fired. Not to fire it would make the gun unnecessary. Not to mention it would create imbalance within the story.

4. **Foreshadowing often takes the form of some detail, incident or clue** mentioned in passing near the beginning of a story, which, once the reader has almost forgotten it, can be given its full significance later.

5. **For instance, if you introduce a character as being from a family historically given to incestuous relationships, with insanity as a by-product,** having a hitherto sane character lose their sanity in the last act would be the result of earlier foreshadowing.

6. **Then there's the 'bad dream' type of foreshadowing,** in which a character expresses a terrible fear of something happening (for instance, becoming like one of their parents), at which point it's almost certainly going to be reflected in the plot.

7. **This idea is nicely subverted in the movie** *Galaxy Quest,* **where Guy is set up from the start as the one most likely to die, but ends up transcending his destiny.** This too is a kind of foreshadowing, but with a twist.

8. **There's also the very common kind of foreshadowing whereby a character who is about to die is given a moment in the spotlight** – an interlude, a little set piece – which, when done properly, helps to add poignancy and meaning to the scene.

9. You can achieve some **nice foreshadowing effects with imagery**: e.g. using darker imagery around someone who is going to die later, or a crown of sunlight on the head of a person destined to be king. Stay subtle, though: a little of that goes a long way.

10. To work, foreshadowing should be approached with delicacy. It's very easy to make it look clunky and obvious. But when a plot feels a little unfinished, some well-placed foreshadowing can be a good way of bringing it all together.

10

Letting Go

So here it is. You've finished your novel. You've edited and rewritten it to the best of your ability, with the help of a competent editor. Now it's time to either submit it to an agent, or to your existing publisher, or maybe to self-publish it online. You should be very proud of yourself. This is the culmination of all your hard work and energy. You're excited to get to the next stage. So why is it so hard to press *Send*?

1. Don't worry. You're not alone. Separation anxiety from a work-in-progress is very real, and is tied in with the fear of rejection, the fear of others reading your work and the fear of not being ready for what comes next.

2. That's one of the many reasons you need a trustworthy editor. They will be able to tell you whether your work is ready for submission or not. It's natural for a writer to want to hang on to their work for a while, but ask yourself whether doing this is really going to improve the book, or whether you're just afraid of going to the next stage.

3. Bear in mind that if you're submitting a manuscript to an agent, you'll probably have to rewrite it a number of times – that's even if you are accepted. You'll have plenty of opportunities to make changes – maybe more changes than you're expecting.

4. Bear in mind, too, that if you don't take your project to the next stage, then this is as far as it can ever go. There's nothing inherently wrong with that – you may be writing for yourself alone – but don't let fear stop you from trying to take it further if you want to.

5. Some writers find that it helps to start working on something new. It takes the edge off the fear of being judged, and allows you to put some distance between you and your anxiety.

6. Sometimes a project needs a period of rest time. This doesn't mean it's dead, but you may need to leave it for a year or longer before you're ready to knock it into shape for submission. If so, work on something else. You'll have something else to offer by the time you're ready.

7. Remind yourself that you have nothing to lose. Whatever happens – even if your book is rejected, even if someone doesn't like it – what you've done is a personal achievement. You deserve to celebrate.

8. Write down how you're feeling. That way next time (because there *will* be a next time) won't seem as gruelling.

9. Understand this: you may *never* feel quite ready to let go. On the other hand, there will come a point when you will need to move on.

10. Remind yourself how it felt to begin writing this story. How nervous you were, how unsure you'd ever make it this far. Then, just as you gave yourself permission to write, give yourself permission to let go. You've worked so hard, you've learnt so much – now you deserve to see what comes next. Whatever it is, you have already achieved more than most people ever will.

PART 7

Who Makes a Book?

Bringing out a book sometimes feels like giving birth. Like giving birth, it's both exhausting and exhilarating in turns. Like giving birth, it's not the end of a process, but the start of a journey. Also, like giving birth, it involves more than just one person.

Whether you're aiming to sell the rights to your book, or to publish it yourself, you're going to need a certain amount of help, whether it's to negotiate your contract with a publisher, to copy-edit your text, help promote and package your book, or just make it look more beautiful.

This section deals with some of the people you're likely to encounter on your journey to publication and beyond (assuming publication is what you want from your writing); including what they do for authors, how they work and why they're important to the process.

1. Agents
2. Publishers
3. Editors
4. Publicists
5. Translators
6. Illustrators and Designers
7. Audiobook Readers
8. Bloggers
9. Booksellers
10. Readers

It can be difficult to give yourself time
to write so consider writing two books
at the same time.

1

Agents

If you're hoping to be published via a traditional route, it's likely you'll need an agent. Agents are the gatekeepers of the publishing world: they work with publishing houses and editors to match the right publisher to the right author, and publishers trust their recommendations.

Often with the help of a specialist team, they will try and get the best deal for your book, as well as going over contracts, negotiating foreign rights, dealing with media, TV and film rights, and advising you on all aspects of your writing career. For this, they take a percentage (usually between 15 per cent and 20 per cent) of the money that comes to you from your publisher.

Many publishers don't accept submissions by unagented authors, and certainly such submissions take longer to be read and considered. Some of the publishers that do may try to get away with giving their authors the kind of contract no agent would allow them to sign. But finding an agent is often as hard as finding a publisher: there are so many agents out there, and they all have different methods and specializations. Their names and contact details are available in publications like *The Writers' and Artists' Yearbook*, and most of them have websites, or are active on social media.

Here are a few guidelines when it comes to approaching them:

1. Do your research before contacting an agent. Not all agents are the same. Some are seasoned veterans, some are young people just building up their client list. Some only represent writers of commercial fiction, others represent only non-fiction, or screenplays, or poetry. Don't waste time sending your three-volume fantasy epic to someone who specializes in representing military historians.

2. Read the agent's submission guidelines. These will usually be available on their website, and will include things like how many sample chapters you should send, what format you should use, and how long you can expect to wait before getting a reply. Read them carefully, and submit accordingly. You won't make a good impression if you can't even follow a set of basic instructions.

3. Some agents don't take unsolicited submissions at all. In that case, don't approach them. Make sure you choose an agent who welcomes unsolicited manuscripts.

4. Avoid any agent who charges a reading fee (or any other kind of fee). Look out for agents who are members of the Association of Authors' Agents (AAA) or similar – this means that they have agreed to a correct and ethical code of practice.

5. Don't approach too many agents at once. No one appreciates a bulk email. Make your approach personal, concise and clear – then wait patiently for a response.

6. Don't expect an answer straightaway. If you haven't had an answer after three months, you may wish to follow up with a polite email or phone call. Three months isn't an unusual time to wait: some agents get hundreds of unsolicited manuscripts a week. It takes time to sift through them. And don't expect a speedy reply over Christmas, the school holidays, or trade events like the Frankfurt Book Fair. Those are busy times for agents, and looking at submissions won't be a priority.

7. **If an agent rejects you, don't argue**, push back or bitch about them on social media. That kind of behaviour does you no favours – and will almost certainly prejudice your next attempt. Thank the agent for their time, and if they give you reasons for their rejection, take note, and be prepared to consider them. It may be that if you write something more to their taste, they will look at your work again. Leave as many options open as you can. And remember, agents *talk* to each other, and they remember *everything*.

8. **As a rule, don't send an unfinished or unedited book to an agent.** Make your manuscript as good as you can possibly make it: after all, you only have one chance to make a first impression, and you will be one of many writers vying for their attention.

9. **While you're waiting for a response, keep on writing.** At best, it will mean that you'll have begun your next novel by the time you get an agent: at the very worst, it means that if your manuscript is rejected, you'll already have moved on to better things.

10. **Don't jump at the first offer from an agent to sign you up.** Meet with them in person; make sure you're on the same wavelength. If you already have an offer from another agent, say so. It's only polite. When you do sign with an agent, tell the others and thank them for their time. And make sure

you *do* sign a contract. That way if you ever need to change agents, you'll know exactly how much notice to give, and how to formalize the change.

Remember, agents are people just like you, trying to make a living. It's up to you to prove yourself worthy of attention, not up to them to 'discover' your talent. And when you *do* get an agent, don't assume you're high and dry. The hard work is just beginning . . .

2

Publishers

In these days of self-publishing, not every writer seeking publication needs a traditional publisher. However, having a publisher is still often the easiest option – a publisher will provide you with editors, copy-editors, proof-readers, publicists, artists, designers, distributors: all of which you'll need to source for yourself if you decide to go it alone. Which is not to say that self-publishing is less valid in any way: it just means a different (and sometimes harder) journey to publication.

Whichever path you eventually choose, it's important to understand what a publisher does, and just what you're actually signing if and when you sign that contract. Basically, when you accept a contract with a publisher, you're *selling them the right to publish your book*; depending on the contract, this may also include other rights, e.g. foreign, audiobook, e-book rights, etc. If you self-publish, you *retain* your rights, which means no one can legally exploit them without your permission.

It's very important to get this stage right: if you sign a contract with a publisher, the relationship you have with them is likely to be one of the most important of your career as an author. Here are a few things to consider before you take the plunge:

1. **Not all publishers are the same**. Some produce e-books only. Some are new and very small. Some are reliant on funding. Some are very large and influential. Either way, when considering a publisher, you'll need to think carefully about what your choice will mean to you.

2. **A big publisher generally has more money, reach and influence**, but unless you're a big-name author, it's sometimes easy to feel lost among the many hundreds of titles they bring out every year. A small press may give you a greater degree of personal attention, but they may only be able to bring out a handful of books a year. Which one would be best for you? That's for you to decide.

3. **Your agent should advise you on the subject of publishers**; but it's also useful to do one's own research. Social media allows for a far greater sharing of information than ever used to be possible: if you're lucky enough to have several offers of publication, don't hesitate to ask around. What have others experienced when dealing with this publisher? How comfortable would you feel working with them?

4. **If possible, meet your publisher. Meet your prospective editor.** Make sure you're going to be comfortable working with them, and that they understand you. Remember, you may be working with them for a long time.

5. **No publisher, however small, should be charging you money to publish**. Beware vanity imprints that expect authors to pay for publication or publicity costs: they seldom deliver the kind of services they promise, and most bookshops won't stock their books. No author should *ever* be

asked to pay a publisher for their services: any company who asks for this isn't really a publisher at all.

That isn't to say that a combination of expert freelancer services and a print-on-demand arrangement service might not be a good idea if what you want is a few dozen copies of your book to give to family and friends. There are several good and reputable companies out there that will do just that. But if you want your books to be *sold*, you'll need a publisher with a sales team. Otherwise, the only way you'll be able to sell your books is through e-retailers like Amazon, or by hand-selling your books wherever you can.

6. Beware of publishers who don't pay authors an advance. If you have an agent, they should have warned you against these people anyway. If you don't, and you're uncertain of the contract you're being asked to sign, run it past the legal team at the Society of Authors – they'll advise you, and if you're a member, they'll do it for free.

7. If ever a situation arises whereby you feel let down by your publisher, go to your agent. That's what they're for: to negotiate – and sometimes to complain – on your behalf, and to preserve good working relations between you and your publisher. If you don't have an agent, go to your trade union (if you have one), the Society of Authors or the Writers' Guild.

8. If your publisher drops you, don't take it personally. It's business: it's not about you. Publishing is a pretty close community, and you'll probably end up meeting them – maybe even working with them – again. Try not to make it awkward.

9. Don't sign rights over to your publishers unless they're able to deal with them. That means media rights, film rights, audio rights, foreign-language rights. There's no point giving these things to your publishers if they're not going to exploit them. If you do sign them away, *never* give them away for free. Even if you think they're worthless now, they may be valuable later.

10. Be aware of your publisher's needs in terms of delivery deadlines, promotion and other commitments. Make sure they're aware of your needs, too. That way, no one in the relationship feels let down, disappointed or under-appreciated.

3

Editors

Whoever you are, and however great your talent, you're going to need an editor. If you're with a traditional publisher, they will pair you up with one who may not be the same person as your acquiring or commissioning editor; if not, you'll have to source one for yourself. There are many freelance editors available online: choose carefully, check out their references, their website (their spelling!), and make sure to check their rates against the Society of Authors' recommended rates before you commit to a working relationship. Your relationship with your editor is crucial to the success of your book, and whoever you end up working with needs to be trustworthy, professional, competent and in tune with the kind of thing you're writing.

1. Book editors don't actually *edit* your work. They read it, assess it and come up with suggestions on how to improve it. It's pretty much up to you to decide whether or not to implement their suggestions – although if you refuse to accept *any* feedback, your publisher may decide your book isn't in a fit state to be published. However, if you trust your editor, you should take their suggestions seriously, even if you don't agree with everything.

2. You will usually have an *editor*, and a *copy-editor*. Your editor's job is to look at the book from a reader's point of view. They will tell you how well your characters come across, whether your plot flows nicely, whether you achieved what you intended. This kind of editor gives you guidelines on rewriting and redrafting your manuscript, rather than focusing on individual words and phrases. This generally comes later, as part of the copy-editing stage.

3. A *copy-editor* will look at your writing line-by-line, will point out misspellings or repeated words, will check time-lines and historical facts, will tell you if something you've written sounds clunky or doesn't make sense. You need both an editor and a copy-editor. Both roles are vital in getting your manuscript ready for publication.

4. If you have a traditional publishing deal try to get to know your commissioning editor. They will often be your first point of contact with your publisher. They often liaise with the publicity, sales and marketing, and art departments, too. They're on your side, to help boost your profile and to keep you in the loop. Meet them, or speak to them on the phone. Follow them on social media. This is one of the most important professional relationships you are likely to have, and it needs to be a good one. They need to believe in you, and you need to understand and respect their views. Otherwise, you're both wasting your time.

5. When your editor has given you their notes, don't comment or react straightaway. Thank your editor for their suggestions, then give yourself a couple of weeks to mull over their ideas. It's normal to want to reject *all* their ideas and criticisms at first; but once you've gained some objectivity, you'll be able to see where your editor may have a point, and where and why you disagree with them.

6. If you're with a traditional publisher and you feel your editor isn't quite on your wavelength, or if you feel they don't have enough time to give you the individual attention you need, you may prefer to also work with an independent editor of your own choosing. That way, you get the advantages of being with a traditional publisher, and the flexibility of independence.

7. A good editor knows when to criticize and when to offer praise. If all your editor ever gives you is praise, they're playing to your vanity. Ditch them.

8. A good editor knows the difference between helping an author write the best book they possibly can, and trying to take creative control. Your editor should never make you feel as if your book isn't yours any more.

9. A good editor reads widely and enthusiastically, and understands (and likes) the genre in which you are writing. Ideally, they also engage with the reading community and are active there on your behalf.

10. Make sure you acknowledge your editor's work. Remember: they're not working *for* you; they're working *with* you. Like all the people who help your book make it into print, they're important, and they deserve credit where it's due.

4

Publicists

Not everyone gets a publicist. If you're traditionally published, though, chances are you'll get one at some point. If not, or if you want more from your publicist than just the standard two or three weeks around the time of publication, you may wish to consider hiring an independent publicist (this needs serious thought, though, and can cost serious money), or doing your own publicity on whatever scale seems appropriate.

1. The job of a publicist is to write press releases, arrange interviews, liaise with media and organize readings and appearances at literary festivals on your behalf. They will also be in charge of sending out advance review copies of your books, and may also organize things like blog tours, guest blog appearances, competitions and anything else designed to raise your profile and sell your book, inasmuch as your publicity budget allows.

2. Most traditionally published authors will get their main publicity around the two weeks or so surrounding the launch of a new book. They will be sharing the services of an in-house publicist, who will also be dealing with a number of other authors. Publicists are notoriously overworked and underappreciated, so don't expect miracles.

3. It's well worth getting your publicist on your side. Talk to them. Make it clear what you're interested (or not interested) in doing. If you really hate public speaking, tell them so, and they'll steer you away from public appearances. If you're interested in blogging or writing for a magazine on a certain subject, tell them so, and they'll find out who may be interested in publishing your article.

4. It helps if you are reasonably active on social media. Make your publicist aware of the things you're doing online that might be helpful – newsletters, websites, blog posts, giveaways. Anything you can do to help will make their job easier, and will improve your chances of visibility.

5. Tell your publicist if you know any other authors, reviewers or bloggers who might be able to help raise the profile of your book. If appropriate, they can then send them review copies. Don't be tempted to do this yourself – it's nearly always better to go through the correct channels.

6. Don't expect your publicist to do all the work on your behalf. Be imaginative. Ask questions. Look at festivals you'd like to attend well in advance, and ask your publicist if there's a chance of you getting a slot.

7. Ideally, certain kinds of publicity should start a long time before publication. Big festivals often schedule their events a year ahead, so be realistic: don't start asking about Hay-on-Wye or Edinburgh three weeks before the festival starts. And if you contribute an article for a magazine to tie in with the release of your book, you'll need to submit it at least three months before the magazine is due to come out.

8. Ask to look over your press release *before* it goes out to the press. Make sure it says everything you want it to say. Ideally, write your own list of things you'd like your press release to include, and make sure your publicist gets it in time. That includes a brief description of your book, any special interests, and anything that makes your book (or you) particularly current, interesting or newsworthy.

9. Depending on your circumstances, your publicist may accompany you on your book tour. In that case, they (as a representative of the publisher) should provide things like rail tickets, meals, accommodation, etc. If that doesn't happen, keep receipts and details of expenses, and give them to your publicist. You shouldn't have to pay your own expenses on a promotional tour.

10. Don't treat your publicist like a dogsbody. Appreciate them. Maybe give them a little gift at the end of your book tour, or send them a personal thank-you note. Too many authors don't do this, and it sucks.

Translators

If you're published in any language other than your own, you'll have a designated translator, and the quality of their work can mean the success or failure of your books. As such, it's worth getting to know as much about them as you can. This isn't always easy.

1. Translation is a specialist job, but publishers don't always give translators the time or resources necessary. That's why anything you can do to make their job easier will benefit both of you.

2. Translators are not just competent linguists. They have to be competent stylists, too. A translated book should read fluidly, and should not contain any undue reminders that it's a translation.

3. Most translators are given only three or four months to translate a book. This means that if they encounter an unusual phrase, they may not always be able to give a lot of thought to *exactly* what the author meant.

4. Many publishers forbid translators from getting in touch with authors directly. This is why, if you want to liaise with your translator, you need to make the first move. Write them a note, via your agent, giving them your contact details and giving permission for them to ask you directly if they have any queries regarding your text. Then, answer their queries as fully as you can. That way, you run fewer risks of mis-translation or misunderstanding.

5. Of course, you don't *have* to do this. Answering queries takes time, and not all authors want to do it. (But those authors only have themselves to blame if something gets lost in translation.)

6. If your book contains colloquialisms, regional dialect, unattributed quotations, song lyrics or anything else that a translator might find obscure, you might want to draw up a **troubleshooting list**. (This also helps with US editors, who sometimes need explanations of regional words and expressions.) Send it to your translator, with a clear explanation of what the terms mean.

7. Not all translators are acknowledged on the front cover of the book. If you have any influence with your publisher, consider trying to make sure their name appears under yours. It's only fair.

8. Unless you tell them otherwise, your translator will translate the Acknowledgements page of your book just as it appears in the original. However, it's easy to include in your initial letter to them a little line of acknowledgement – *Thank you to my wonderful translator, [insert your name here]* – and ask them to include it in their country's edition, as well as the names of your foreign editor, cover artist, etc.

9. It's unlikely that you will get a choice of translator, and you may not be fluent in the languages your books are translated into. But if you're on social media, you can sometimes get an impression of what people are saying about your book, and whether they feel the translation is a good one. It's worth doing this if you can, and sending the feedback to your publisher.

10. There's only so much you can do to control the quality of your translated books. Once you've done all you can, let it go. But if feedback tells you that your translations are consistently poor, bring it up with your agent, and consider changing your foreign publisher.

6

Illustrators and Designers

The right illustrator can make a book, just as the wrong one can sink it. Illustrators deserve appreciation, and are often left out – even by the publisher – when it comes to reviews and interviews. It's up to you to make sure that doesn't happen; and remember, someone who feels appreciated by an author is more likely to pull out all the stops on their behalf.

1. Originally, illustrations weren't just for children. From about the 18th century, almost all novels had some illustrations. And recently, beautifully illustrated books for adults have started to return to the mainstream, making hardbacks more desirable, more collectible – and more saleable.

2. Interior illustrations enhance the reading experience by making people read more slowly, and with greater engagement. **Cover design** serves as the reader's first introduction to the book, and is meant to convey the mood, genre and style of the book.

3. As a traditionally published author, you'll become aware that cover art is sometimes created by a different artist to the illustrator. There's also a designer, who takes the cover artwork or photography and uses it to create a complete book jacket. These things all take expertise – and things like fonts, spacing, even the texture of the cover, are all thought out very carefully.

4. If you're a self-published author, you might want to hire someone to do these things for you. Unless you have previous experience in this very specialist skill, chances are you just won't be aware of what it takes to create a professional book jacket. An amateurish jacket design can make a good book look cheesy, and may well put off your readers.

5. Traditionally-published authors don't always have much of a say regarding their cover art. Authors of illustrated books tend to have a closer relationship with their illustrator. But in either case, relationships don't happen by accident. They need work. Build a rapport with your publisher's art department from an early stage, and you're likely to find it easier to become involved in the artistic process.

6. If you're sensitive to cover art, try to get a consultation clause written into your publishing contract. That means you get a certain amount of say regarding your book jackets – including the chance to veto a cover you really don't like.

7. That said, don't be a diva. Your art department consists of professionals who have been doing their job for a long time. If you feel lukewarm about a design that they all agree is terrific, perhaps you should assume that maybe they know more than you do.

8. Get involved with the creative process early, if you're going to be involved at all. Don't be the kind of author that looks at a completed piece of commissioned art and goes: 'That's not what I had in mind.'

9. If you work closely with an illustrator, try not to be a control freak. Talk to them, by all means; tell them how you visualize your characters, but also give them the chance to be creative in their own way, according to their own process.

10. Don't tacitly accept the credit for your illustrator's work. If you've written a book that relies heavily on an illustrator's work for its appeal, make sure you mention your illustrator's name in interviews, and urge reviewers to do the same.

7

Audiobook Readers

If your book is traditionally published, it may be that at some point it will come out as an audiobook. Unless you read it yourself (which sometimes happens, but not usually), it will be recorded by a performer chosen to represent you. As with translations, the quality of this performance may make a big difference to its success, or otherwise.

1. Audiobooks often used to be heavily abridged. Now, with digital media dominating the market, most audiobooks are full-length, and better for it.

2. Audiobooks are big business, and gaining in popularity all the time. Make sure your contract reflects this, and you haven't accidentally signed up all your digital rights to your publisher for nothing (see Know Your Rights in Part 9).

3. Audiobook readers are nearly always professional actors, chosen for their ability to bring different characters to life. Some may be familiar names; others may be unknown to you, but well-known in the audiobook world. Most readers take three to five days to record an average-length audiobook.

4. If you're sensitive to voices and would like a say in the casting of your audiobook reader, it's a good idea to make sure your publishers are aware of this early, so they can involve you in the process. Your publisher may then send you samples of the reader's work, so that you can decide if they're the right reader for your book.

5. Some readers will allocate accents and vocal mannerisms to characters in an attempt to make them stand out better. If you can, you might want to discuss this with them beforehand, rather than be surprised that your protagonist has suddenly turned Welsh overnight.

6. As with translators, if there's anything about your text that may be tricky, it helps to make your reader aware of it. Difficult-to-pronounce names, bits of Old Norse, dialect words – a quick explanatory phone call, or a sound file, emailed to your publisher's audio department, can sometimes be very helpful.

7. If you've written a series of books, it really helps to stick with the same audiobook reader for all of them. It gives continuity to the audience, and confidence to the reader. That's why it's especially important to choose the right reader from the start.

8. Try walking in your audiobook reader's shoes. Practise reading your work aloud. It can really help you work out any problems you may have with the fluency of your written style; and if your style is fluid and easy to read, it will enhance your likelihood of getting an audiobook deal.

9. Audiobooks, like e-books, are frequently pirated online. Help yourself and your audiobook reader by regularly reporting any incidents of piracy to your publisher and getting your work taken down.

10. As with illustrators and translators, it really helps to thank your audiobook reader for their work, either with a personal note, or with a few words on social media. They will appreciate it, and it will help you with any future projects.

8

Bloggers

Since the decline of print media, book bloggers (and YouTubers, and Instagrammers) have become very influential in terms of generating interest in books and reading. Publicists often contact them with review copies and offers of guest posts, and they are very often the first port of call for self-published authors wanting to get their books reviewed. Here are a few guidelines on what to expect from the blogging community, and what you should be offering in return.

1. Not all book bloggers are the same. Some have a large following and an interesting approach to reviewing; others, not so much. But book blogging is a community and, both as readers and as authors, we owe this community a great deal. Check out the blogs that cater to your tastes; find out whose opinions you respect. That way you can interact with the online book community in a mutually beneficial way.

2. A good review on a prominent, well-respected blog can really help publicize an author's work. But always remember that's not what they're for. They can certainly benefit authors, but they exist to enable *readers* to find the books they're likely to enjoy.

3. Don't send out review copies indiscriminately to every blogger you can think of. Find out whether your book is a good fit for their blog, and whether your chosen genre is the kind of thing they're likely to read.

4. Book bloggers are not paid for their work in the way print reviewers are paid. They are enthusiastic amateurs, and as such they don't owe you a review, even if you send them a book.

5. Nor do they owe you a *good* review. A reputable blogger will write an honest review in exchange for an advance reader copy from the publisher or author.

6. The online organizations selling five-star reviews to the needy and desperate are not genuine book bloggers, and people in the business know to give them a wide berth. The world is full of crooks waiting to prey on authors, and paying for fake reviews online is just a waste of your money.

7. If you're a self-published author hoping to be reviewed by a blogger, **don't start out by asking for a review. Engage with them first.** Read their blog. Subscribe to their newsletter. Talk to them online. Show interest, rather than just self-interest.

8. If a blogger gives you a good review, return the favour if you can. That might mean writing a guest post, or recommending them for a blogger award, or giving them an exclusive interview. People who only dip into the pool when they think they'll benefit don't tend to last long in the community.

9. Don't complain if a blogger gives you a bad review, or doesn't get round to reviewing you at all. That happens sometimes. It's not their job to help publicize your books; they *choose* to do what they do. And if you're rude or objectionable, you can be sure they won't recommend you to anyone else in future.

10. Most bloggers like to talk to authors online, meet them at conventions and generally hang out. However, a few are nervous of author contact, preferring to keep their blog for readers only. Make sure before you reach out that you're not invading someone's space.

9

Booksellers

In spite of the growing popularity of online retailers, a good high-street or local independent bookseller is worth their weight in gold. It's worth befriending your local ones, and not just because they can help you.

1. A good bookseller knows their customers, and can help match readers with the books they will love.

2. Booksellers can organize readings, book launches and other author events that will help you reach out to readers within the community.

3. Independent bookshops are in decline: the ones that remain are generally run by people who are passionate about reading, and are often filled with great ideas to help promote sales.

4. High-street bookshops are also in decline: they too are suffering from competition with the online retailers. Authors can support both high-street bookshops like Waterstones, *and* smaller independents, by agreeing to do a variety of signings, readings and publicity events.

5. Discount bookshops are not your friends: they sell books at such reduced prices that other booksellers find it hard to survive alongside them; and the royalties earned by the authors from such cheap sales amount to barely a handful of change.

6. The display slots in larger retailers are often bought and paid for by the publishers as part of an author's promotion campaign. That's why the books in seasonal promotions, special displays or with discounted offers are often by big-name authors.

7. Smaller, independent bookshops have no such restrictions over what they can display, and where. That's why it's a good idea to get to know your local independent bookseller. If they like you, they can display your book prominently, or recommend it to readers they think will enjoy it.

8. Distributing advance reader copies to friendly booksellers before the publication of your book may result in them ordering more copies in, or, if they like it, recommending it to their customers.

9. If you do a public reading or a signing in a bookshop, the bookseller will order more copies of your book in order to meet the extra demand. If those copies aren't all sold, the bookshop usually has the option of returning them to the publisher. But if you sign the stock for them, it usually won't be returned and will sell quickly.

10. If you do a reading or other kind of book event in a library, church hall or similar, you may want to get in touch with a local bookseller, in order to get them to sell books on your behalf. This is where having a good relationship with a local independent bookseller comes in handy. Both of you will benefit from the added sales and trust me, lugging boxes of books to events and trying to sell them yourself isn't a good look for any author.

10

Readers

Whether you're a published author, or simply wanting to hone your style, it's essential to remember who you're doing all this *for*. Writing for an audience is about reaching out to other people; it promotes the sharing of ideas; it makes a lasting connection between the reader and the writer.

In such a crowded marketplace, and with so many other writers, all of them vying for readers too, it's important not to take your reader's attention for granted, or assume that when you have it, they'll stay with you for the journey. So here are ten things about the most important relationship a writer can have: the one they have with their audience.

1. Readers don't owe you anything. It's up to you to draw them in. After that, it's a question of keeping their attention, of making them want to turn the page.

2. Don't blame the readers if your book fails to engage them. It's not their fault.

3. Don't work from an ivory tower. Make a human connection. If you're on social media, don't just try to promote your books: show your readers something that makes them feel that you have something in common: a shared passion, a secret, a fear; a special way of seeing the world. If that happens, your readers will want to know more about you.

4. Respect your readers. That means giving them the best you can give – in terms of writing, editing and research. They'll know if you're being lazy or cutting corners, and they'll judge you accordingly.

5. Remember that your readers may be diverse in all kinds of ways. Be inclusive: try to acknowledge some of that diversity in your writing.

6. Don't assume the public is stupid. There's nothing worse than a patronizing author trying to replicate a popular trend. And authors who write from a position of assumed superiority rarely succeed.

7. If you engage with readers, do it in public, and in your own space. Use your social media platforms; your website if you have one. Never use reader platforms like Goodreads or Amazon to engage with readers about your books, however much you are tempted to do so.

8. Don't argue with your readers. You can't force them to like your book, or understand what you meant to say. All you can do is give them your book, say: *I made this for you, with love*, and wait to see what happens.

9. No one at your publisher's will *force* you to interact with your readers, either on social media or by attending book events. But without the readers, your book would stay unread. **Acknowledge the debt you owe them.** Go to readings, festivals and conventions. Engage online. Answer questions about your work. But for your own safety, keep a respectful distance between yourself and the public – there may be the occasional person out there who needs to be kept at arm's length.

10. All readers are different. However successful or well-written your book, some people just won't like it. Don't take criticism personally: no one, however good they are, can escape it. It's part of being a writer.

PART 8

Why Am I Doing This, Again?

This section is for that inevitable moment when you start to wonder whether you're ever going to achieve your objective; whether that's getting an agent, a publisher, a greater number of readers or just a satisfactory first draft. Writing can be joyous, but it's also deeply frustrating. This is for those days when your frustration eclipses your joy. I've been though every one of these stages, and so have most authors you've heard of. So grit your teeth, make a cup of tea, take a deep breath, and read on . . .

1. What Makes a Bestseller?

2. Why Can't I Get an Agent?

3. Why Was My Manuscript Rejected?

4. Why Shouldn't I Just Publish Myself?

5. Why Does Everything Take So Long?

6. How Can I Make More Money From My Writing?

7. How Can I Promote My Books?

8. How Can I Get Reviews?

9. Why Are So Many Terrible Books Bestsellers?

10. Will a Creative Writing Course Help Me Succeed?

Write something – anything – every day.
For example, yesterday I wrote a letter.
It was a 'b', but I wasn't happy
with it so I changed it to a 'p'.

1

What Makes a Bestseller?

Who *doesn't* want their books to reach the widest possible audience? If any of us knew for sure exactly how to write a bestseller, then we'd be doing it all the time. If *publishers* automatically knew what made a bestseller, then there wouldn't be so many surprise bestsellers out there. But there *are* a number of things that a lot of bestsellers have in common. Here they are.

1. It helps to be genuinely passionate about your subject matter. Books written in response to trends or market analyses are very seldom really successful. But passion generates passion.

2. To have a beautiful written style is always nice. But to have a damn good story is essential.

3. Books written on a number of different levels generally appeal to a larger group of readers. A really good story, enriched by interesting and well-drawn characters, a strong authorial voice and some thought-provoking themes will cover a lot of bases. That's how Hilary Mantel manages to write prize-winning literary fiction that also appeals to a mass audience.

4. We read to escape our everyday lives. A bestseller generally gives the reader the opportunity to enter a world that they *really* want to visit.

5. Most bestsellers feature **a character** that readers will find either very likeable, very interesting, very memorable or very relatable.

6. A bestseller generally features **a concept, idea or theme** that the reader hasn't met in that form before. Doing something for the second or third time isn't enough to catch the zeitgeist.

7. Bestsellers nearly always have **a balance between the familiar and the unfamiliar.** However fantastical the situation, the readers need to be able to imagine themselves in it. For example, Harry Potter: a quite ordinary boy in an extraordinary environment.

8. No author, critic or publisher gets to decide whether a book will be a bestseller. Only the readers can do that.

9. A bestseller, however happily or tragically it ends, must do so in a way that leaves the reader feeling emotionally satisfied by the journey.

10. Bestsellers exist in all genres, including (but not exclusive to) romance, sci-fi, fantasy, crime, thrillers, children's books, YA and literary fiction. Genre doesn't matter. What matters is what your book achieves, and how the public receives it.

2

Why Can't I Get an Agent?

Getting an agent is often as difficult and as lengthy a process as finding a publisher. Some writers try to bypass this stage, but I wouldn't advise it if you're aiming for a traditional publishing deal. For publishers, agents exist as the first line of defence against a barrage of new manuscripts sent out by writers every day. They filter out the ones they think don't have a chance of being published, consider some of the ones that do, and take on the authors they really believe they can represent. It's often frustrating trying to find an agent who will represent you, and it can be tempting to see these gatekeepers as angry gamekeepers trying to keep you out of the enchanted forest of publishing, rather than hardworking professionals, trying to make sure the forest isn't overrun by noisy tourists with picnic-baskets who don't know the rules.

1. Yes, sometimes agents make mistakes. But if you've applied to numerous agents, and been rejected every time, chances are you need to look again, either at your approach, or your manuscript.

2. Perhaps you're just not ready. It's hard to know for sure when it's time to submit a manuscript, and some writers are eager to approach agents and publishers before their book is in a publishable state. Remember, you're not on a deadline. You have the luxury of time. Use it well, and don't rush in. Make your first impression count.

3. Finding an agent is a bit like applying for a job: you may not get the job every time, but if you don't even get interviews, there's probably something lacking in your skill set. Consider sending a sample of your work to a manuscript evaluator or freelance editor, who should be able to give you advice on how to move forward.

4. Try politely asking for feedback. Some agents don't have time for this, but any amount of advice you get – however small – can be valuable.

5. If you're lucky enough to get detailed advice from an agent, ask them if they would be prepared to look at your manuscript again once you've made the necessary changes. If they agree, that's great: it's a sign you're getting somewhere.

6. Don't go back to an agent unless you really *have* implemented their suggestions. Many writers think that they can get away with a few token changes and tweaks before resubmitting. Don't waste the opportunity: at this stage, you need to demonstrate the ability to take advice and to act upon it. But if you really work with their suggestions, you'll have the chance to impress them.

7. Don't be tempted to 'cut out the middle-man'. Sometimes, at this stage, a writer may start to feel very jaded, and try to approach publishers directly. Don't. If you can't impress an agent, you won't impress a publisher, either. And there are plenty of sharks in the form of vanity presses masquerading as small publishers, waiting for you to reach this stage and hand them all your money. Publishing is filled with middle-men. You need to prove you can work with them.

8. At this stage, it's hard to be patient. And yet, more patience is just what you need. Avoid giving yourself dead-lines (*I need to get an agent by this time next year; I need to write a bestseller before I'm thirty*): they only lead you into patterns of negative thinking.

9. Reassess your ambitions. Ask yourself what you *really* want. Is it really to be a *professional* writer? If so, why? If the answer is money, remind yourself that the average profes-sional writer earns less than a Starbucks' barista. Then ask yourself this: if you knew you would *never* be published, would you still keep writing? If the answer is no, then maybe reconsider your priorities.

10. Don't lash out at the industry. This is worth saying again, simply because so many people do. No, publishers don't always know *everything*. Sometimes they make mis-takes. But if you really want to be part of the traditional publishing world, you have to understand their rules and work with professionals in the business. If you don't, that's fine, of course – but you can't inhabit two worlds at once.

3

Why Was My Manuscript Rejected?

Rejection happens to all of us. Regardless of success, it never stops being a possibility. And let's not pretend it doesn't suck: it does, and it never gets easier. But rejection is a necessary and inevitable part of any author's journey, and it can offer useful insights. First, it helps to try to identify *why* your book was rejected.

1. Maybe your book wasn't ready to submit. Agents and publishers often don't have the resources to knock an unfinished book into shape, especially if it's by a newcomer. If it looks as if significant editorial work needs to be done on a first novel, chances are they'll pass.

2. Maybe you chose the wrong person to send it to. Agents and publishers often deal with certain genres only: if your work falls outside their area of specialization, they'll probably not engage.

3. Maybe it's the wrong time for your book to be published. Either the market is saturated with similar ideas; or maybe yours is too different from the mainstream. Either way, don't despair. Try something else. But don't ditch your original project: its time may come.

4. Maybe your project wasn't seen to be commercial enough. This is often the case with books by unknown authors. It's not enough to just be good: it takes a really strong idea to break through. In that case, try again with something else. Your backlist may get its chance later.

5. Maybe it just wasn't good enough. This is the hardest one to accept; but even so, sometimes it happens. If you think this is the case, you'll need to identify what your weaknesses are as a writer, and work on improving them. We're learning new skills all the time: yours may need developing.

6. Or maybe your book *was* good enough, but whoever read it just didn't see its potential. The bestseller list is filled with books that were rejected at the outset. Publishers are only human, and sometimes, humans make mistakes. If so, someone will pick your book up eventually. It's just a matter of time and persistence.

7. Maybe you're using the wrong approach. Most traditional publishers don't accept submissions other than through an agent. Publishers just don't have the staff to read through every unsolicited manuscript, and rely on agents to advise them on whether a book will suit them. If you send your manuscript to publishers without going through an agent, your work is likely to be overlooked.

8. Maybe your book is too long. First novels should ideally be between 80,000 and 100,000 words. Anything much longer than this is probably too bulky, and needs paring down; anything less will be too slight.

9. Maybe your book is too difficult to categorize. Most publishers like to be able to fit a book into a specific genre: it helps to market it to the readers. Novels that cross over genres – though they are becoming more acceptable – are still seen as a bit of a risk.

10. Either way, whatever the reason your book was rejected, don't take it personally. It's not because you're being picked on, or blocked, or because publishers are mean, or the public stupid. Dust yourself off, and try again. We've all been there.

4

Why Shouldn't I Just Publish Myself?

Well, of course, you absolutely *can*. But there's no 'just' about it. Self-publishing commercially is at least as demanding and difficult as going down the traditional route. It will cost you money, too, if you do it properly. But self-published books are now potentially as well-respected as traditional books, and are likely to become even more popular.

Of course, just how much you put into your self-publishing project depends on what you hope to achieve. If what you want is the chance to see your novel online, get feedback, share your ideas, or even have a few dozen copies of your memoir printed for your family, then yes, go ahead. Self-publishing works. But if you want to sell your books, get more than a handful of readers, maybe even earn a decent amount of money from your work, then you'll need to put at least as much work into self-publishing as you would going down the traditional route. That's because traditional publishers provide their authors with editors, copy-editors, designers, proof-readers, publicists and everything they need to make the book as successful and polished as it can be. If you choose to self-publish, you will have to do all that your-self – or find someone who can.

Finding someone who can is nearly always the best option, given the fact that all these are professional, specialist skills. And specialists and professionals need to be paid – which means that self-publishing will cost you money up front that you may never be sure of getting back. It can be done. It can even be done very successfully – Hugh Howey is an excellent example of a self-published author who reached the best-seller lists by dint of hard work and persistence. And many big publishers are now looking at successful self-published authors, and offering them traditional book deals. But do not underestimate the difficulty of this route. It isn't an easy option. Nor is it generally possible to have your books trans-lated or released as audiobooks if you choose this option. But it can be used to good effect, just as long as you bear these things in mind:

1. The temptation is to cut corners. Don't. You may well have a readership out there, hoping for a book just like yours. Traditional publishing is risk-averse, and a book considered too risky, too niche, may well find its audience online. But you still need to make sure your book is polished and profes-sional. You owe it to your readers. And that means putting in the same amount of work in terms of editing, proofing, promotion, etc. as any traditionally published writer.

2. Don't mistake self-publishing with vanity publishing. They are not at all the same thing. There are many dif-ferences; the main one being that self-publishing is not exploitative: vanity publishing is. Vanity publishers never come out and admit they're vanity publishers. Many of them actually specify they're not, and present themselves as small presses instead. However, there are a number of warning signs you can look for to identify them. The main one is that no reputable publisher will ever ask an author for money in exchange for publication. Follow the money, and beware.

3. Vanity publishers are more likely to advertise their services in magazines and online. They tend to target older people, so you'll often find their advertising in magazines like *Saga* and *The Oldie*. They can be very plausible, but before you fall for their spiel, know this. Real publishers don't need to go touting for business. Real publishers pay the author, not the other way around.

4. Although self-published authors may incur costs for services like editing, design, etc., these services' costs are relatively low – in the hundreds, rather than thousands. Vanity publishers often charge many thousands of pounds for what is basically a very overpriced print-on-demand service.

5. Vanity publishers often make unfounded claims, promising to distribute the author's books, to organize tours, festival appearances, etc. However, most bookshops won't stock vanity-published books, and festivals don't invite vanity-published writers.

6. Vanity publishers often advertise 100 per cent royalties, as if this is a good thing. All it means is you get to keep 100 per cent of the sale price of the book YOU HAVE ALREADY PAID FOR.

7. Vanity publishers often claim to offer editorial services. Most of the time, however, these are just a means of making the author feel validated and important. They won't risk making real editorial suggestions for fear of putting off their customers.

8. Vanity publishers often advertise themselves as accepting unrepresented authors. This is not a good thing – it's just because no worthwhile agent would ever allow their author to be exploited in this way.

9. Vanity presses are exploitative, not because they allow people to publish their own books, but because they pretend to offer so much more than just a printing service. **There's nothing wrong with wanting to get a few copies of your book printed for yourself, or for your family.** But there are lots of ways you can get this done cheaply, using a number of online printing resources, and without falling prey to a vanity press.

10. No book promotes itself, whether it's self-published or not. If you want your self-published book to reach the greatest possible readership, you'll need to work on your online audience long before you start. That means spending time building your social media platforms, engaging with the online reading community, blogging, guest blogging, posting videos on YouTube, interacting with other writers and generally building your profile. This can take time. Once again, you need to prepare for the long haul.

5

Why Does Everything Take So Long?

Everything in publishing takes so much longer than you think it will. Finding an agent, getting a deal, waiting for a book to come out. That's why it's important that you *enjoy* the process of writing: everything moves at a snail's pace, and things don't necessarily speed up after your first novel is published. Writing books is a long game, but if you *really enjoy* what you do, your love of writing will sustain you through frustrations, rejections, bad patches. This section is for anyone who has ever wondered just where all the time goes.

1. You should always give an edit or rewrite all the time it needs. If you're not with a publisher, you have the luxury of time. Use it to the maximum: once you've been signed up, I guarantee you'll never have that luxury again.

2. If you *are* with a publisher, try to give them an accurate idea of when you'll get the work to them. Publishers are usually more understanding when they know a long time in advance when an author will be able to deliver. That's because the process involves lots of other people, who will be left twiddling their thumbs if you don't work to schedule.

3. **When submitting work to an agent for the first time, expect to hear from them in 3 to 6 months**. That's the amount of time it takes for the average agent's assistant to go through the average slush pile. Think about it: literary agencies often get from 50–300 unsolicited manuscripts *per week*. That's on top of all the agency's existing clients. Each manuscript has to be evaluated. Then, if the book seems to have potential, the reader will write a report for the agent. That process may take several days – and that's for just one manuscript. Multiply that by 300 or more, and you'll see why it takes time.

4. **It's normal to have to wait up to three months or more for an editor to get back to you with their notes**. That's because most editors don't work alone: they often have readers to help them get a broader overview of what your manuscript needs. The more people are involved in a process, the more time it takes.

5. **Most books take at least a year, from the moment of signing the contract, to the moment when they are published**. This is not because a publisher needs a year to publish a book (when a book needs to come out *very* fast, it can always be managed). But publishers like to plan ahead, to look at what other books are likely to come out at the same time, to manage their advance promotion, to take time over the cover art. Look on the bright side: during that time, you could have written the first draft of another book . . .

6. **It's often frustrating that publishers seem to want our edits and rewrites back almost by return of post, whereas when it comes to things that the *author* wants, the process takes so much longer**. That's because the more people are

involved in any process, the longer it takes. Be grateful: you have a team on your side. Give them the chance to do their job.

7. **Similarly, the cover art of a book** seems to take almost as much time to design and to agree as the book itself. That's because it's not only up to the artist and designer to agree and to work on: there's often a whole series of discussions with representatives of book chains – and in some cases, supermarkets – before a final decision is made.

8. **Translations take a surprisingly short time**, compared to other parts of the process. Even so, it can seem like for ever before foreign editions start to come out. This is sometimes because foreign publishers are waiting to see how well a book does in the UK before they decide to publish it themselves. The better your book does in its country of origin, the more likely it is to come out (eventually) elsewhere.

9. **American editions often come out some time later than UK editions.** This can be for all kinds of reasons, but it's often because US editions are edited differently. You're likely to be asked to go through the editorial process again, with a different editor, and a different set of page proofs (likely as not, incorporating US spellings).

10. **Advance payments to authors usually come in slices**: on delivery, on publication, then on publication of the paperback edition. Whether publishers pay these on time really depends on the publisher. I find that some foreign publishers sometimes tend to be *very* late – sometimes long after the publication of a book – but that's one of the reasons we have agents to chase them!

6

How Can I Make More Money From My Writing?

Making money as a writer of fiction is getting harder and harder to achieve. To date, though publishing in general is making more money than ever, authors' income is no higher than it was ten years ago. The average full-time author still earns considerably less than the minimum wage from writing, and many authors have either a supportive partner, or another job on which they rely for their main income. But for now, here are some ideas on how to expand your income doing what you love.

1. Fiction isn't everything. With the right attitude and some contacts, you may be able to create a niche for yourself along-side your fiction writing, working for businesses which may not have the narrative skills to bring to the job.

2. Be prepared to be flexible. Barry Hutchinson (author of the series *BEN 10*) speaks of his numerous false starts and disappointments before finding his niche with a continuing series of children's books. Now, with 120 books in print, most of his income still comes from school visits and talks.

3. It really pays to diversify. Smaller projects add up, and to combine fiction, non-fiction, comics, talks, articles, ghost-writing, visits and corporate events is a good way to get your name out, make contacts and make your writing into a full-time job.

4. If this sounds like a lot of hard work, it is. But no one who goes into writing should expect it to be easy money.

5. A lot of people who want to write for a living imagine that they're going to be working for themselves straightaway. The truth is that as in many other jobs, you pay your dues, learn new skills and gain valuable experience by working for other people first.

6. Hang on to your rights as much as you can. That means digital, audio, TV and film, serialization, foreign rights, VR, game, and anything else that can be used to monetize your IP. There's a lot of money to be made in intellectual property. Make sure some of it goes to you.

7. There's money in social media. Companies will often pay enterprising young writers to blog, tweet or Instagram on their behalf.

8. Rid yourself of the concept that writing should be 'pure', unless you're happy for yours to be largely unpaid.

9. Engaging with the reading and writing community has become essential in raising a new author's profile. Crowdfunding through platforms like Patreon and Ko-fi can help raise money for projects with online publishers like Unbound.

10. Make sure that as soon as you're published, you enter all your books, articles, e-books, audiobooks etc. into the Public Lending Right (PLR) scheme, which pays you a small amount for every time your work is borrowed from a public library. And make sure you join the Authors' Licensing and Collecting Service, which will collect money on your behalf for secondary copyright usage here and overseas. It's your money: you're entitled to it. Make sure it comes home to you!

7

How Can I Promote My Books?

Promotion is something that some writers take to quite easily, and others find very difficult to approach. Writers can be quite reluctant to talk about themselves, and they are often embarrassed at thinking of their work as a product to be sold. Nevertheless, that's what it is, and we all need to work with that.

1. Most traditionally published authors don't get much publicity from their publishers. Even the ones who do get a decent budget can usually benefit from doing some DIY promotion.

2. Independent and self-published writers already know this. But traditional authors can sometimes be unrealistic in their assumptions regarding their publisher's role in promoting their books. (When I asked my first publisher – Warner – about the promotion budget for my first book, they laughed and said: 'Well, we could probably run to a book of stamps.' I got the message.)

3. Here's the thing: **Big publishers are responsible for a lot of authors.** It's unrealistic to expect them to be as aware of your needs as you are. And if your book doesn't get enough attention, they won't blame themselves: they'll blame your book.

4. Of course, no one needs to self-promote if they really don't want to. But it can really help if you do, and it doesn't have to be expensive. Spending money can sometimes help, but using your imagination is better.

5. Become an expert in your field. Have you written a book about an opera singer? Post about opera on social media. Write reviews of performances. Volunteer to write articles and blog posts about your chosen subject. In time, people will start to associate you with that subject. Then, when your book comes out at last, you'll be in a good position to talk about it.

6. Engage with the reading, writing and blogging communities. By this, I don't mean go around shouting 'BUY MY BOOK!' at everyone you meet online (there's a reason it's called 'social' media). But if you support other writers, they'll return the favour.

7. Engage with your local community. Befriend local librarians, English teachers, booksellers, journalists. If you're generous with your time, people may reciprocate.

8. You'll need a website. Yes, I know this is a basic piece of advice, but it's astonishing how many writers don't do this. Publishers' websites, even the good ones, are often rather corporate. Your website should be welcoming, informative and personal: the go-to place on the internet for everything to do with you and your books.

9. Create a newsletter to engage with your readers. Encourage people to sign up by offering exclusive content, giveaways, or competitions. A good newsletter can really help to drive pre-sales, which ensures your book more attention and a higher place in the charts.

10. Don't wait until your book comes out to start promoting it. You'll need to start building momentum months before the release – through cover reveals, blog posts, video clips, teasers – so that when it finally comes out, your readers will be as excited as you are.

8

How Can I Get Reviews?

Everyone likes good reviews: it's a way of getting valida-tion. But online reviews can really drive sales, especially on Amazon and Goodreads, where certain algorithms come into play after a certain number of reviews, enabling your book to appear more visible and more accessible to readers. Still, it's worth bearing a few things in mind before you start.

1. Don't make reviewing all about you. Reviews don't exist primarily to promote the author, but to help readers find the books they'll enjoy.

2. Don't be tempted by websites offering to review your book for money. Paying for a five-star review is as point-less as paying for Twitter followers. They're worthless, and everyone knows it.

3. Don't make your first contact with a blogger or BookTuber a request for a review. You can't expect to be part of a com-munity unless you've engaged with them properly first. So, make friends, comment on their blogs, subscribe to their newsletters. No one owes you a review, especially if you're not willing to put in at least as much as you receive from the writing community. So pay your dues and be generous: that way people are more likely to take an interest in you.

4. Don't send out unsolicited copies of your book to all and sundry. Especially don't send them directly to authors: most authors already get lots of review copies from their publishers and agents. If you particularly want to send a copy to an author, go via their publicist or agent.

5. Do some research. **Send your advance review copies (ARC) to bloggers and publications that may have a special interest in your book.** Does your book feature an autistic protagonist? Steam engines? A cult nineties computer game? Somebody, somewhere, will be discussing the subject behind your passion project. Find them. Join the discussion.

6. Don't expect a review for every ARC you send out. Some well-known bloggers may receive dozens – even hundreds – of ARCs every week. It's up to them whether they review your book at all – and even if they do, of course, they may not give it the five stars you'd like to see!

7. Of course, reviews aren't everything. A photo of your book on someone's Instagram or Twitter could be just as useful as a review in raising awareness.

8. Never fight back over a review, even if you think it's mean or unfair. This is not a fight you can ever win, and the bad vibes you collect will spread across the whole of the writing community.

9. Reviews in local newspapers aren't often very prominent – there's just not enough money to pay a dedicated reviewer – but if you send out a short press release with a blurb you may find that they're willing to use it in their Arts section.

10. Don't forget bookshop staff – if you befriend your local independent bookseller and send them an early copy of your book, they'll help spread the word to their customers if they themselves enjoy it.

9

Why Are So Many Terrible Books Bestsellers?

This is a question I hear a lot from frustrated writers. *Why was that book so successful? It wasn't even well-written. How could it have sold so many copies? Why that book, and not mine?*

I get it. The book market is a strange and mysterious one, and it's not uncommon to see a book that *you* consider trashy and badly written hit the bestseller charts, when something really complex and beautiful fails to gain recognition. It's easy in such cases to slip into negative patterns of thinking; to blame the public, or the industry, or to assume there's some sinister plot at work.

But here's the thing. Fiction is like food: not everyone likes the same thing. And though one item on the menu may be objectively of higher quality than another (a fillet steak as opposed to a cheeseburger), sometimes you just want the cheeseburger anyway. Books are not unlike this. And the book business aims to provide the reading public with a wide variety of different tastes, including things *you* may judge to be of lesser quality. If that seems unfair, then consider the following:

1. **There is no such thing as an objectively terrible best-seller.** That pulpy thriller? That bondage romance? That cheesy police procedural? That ghostwritten kids' book that won an award for the celebrity whose name appeared on the cover, and not the writer who ghosted it? *All of those projects were approved by a group of industry professionals who believed in them.* No publisher will bring out a project they don't believe in. They saw potential for sales in those books, which is why they took them on. And if the book turned out to be a bestseller, *they were right.*

2. **No amount of publicity can make people buy a book they don't want.** Yes, publicity *can* help sales, but the industry is filled with examples of would-be bestsellers that just didn't capture the public imagination in spite of the shed-loads of money spent on them. So, no, bestseller status isn't just a question of publicity.

3. **That goes for celebrity-written books, too.** Remember Madonna's children's book? No? That's because it tanked. Celebrity status alone isn't enough to ensure a book is a bestseller, although yes, in the current climate, publishers *are* more likely to sign up a celebrity than someone you've never heard of. But that doesn't mean their book will sell. For every David Walliams, there are a dozen Madonnas.

4. **It's true that people are more likely to buy a book by an author they know than by an author they've never heard of.** But even bestselling authors need to stay at the top of their game. You know those well-established authors, whose books always seem to jump to the top of the best-seller lists? That process isn't automatic. They've spent years – sometimes decades – putting in the work to ensure

that this will happen. And though that may *look* effortless, it never is.

5. People enjoy and read books for all kinds of reasons. Maybe they love the exciting plot. Maybe they like the characters. Maybe they like a book because it makes them think about something in a new way. And sometimes, it's the language: the way the sentences are crafted. On the other hand, they may be the kind of reader who doesn't care or notice the language: perhaps they're so immersed in the fictional world of the writer that they never think of their style at all. Not everyone notices whether or not a writer uses too many adverbs in their dialogue, and if the story is engaging enough, maybe it doesn't matter.

6. But what about fine writing? I hear you say. Well, some beautiful, complex books *do* make it into the bestseller lists. But not everyone sees fine writing as a priority. You can buy a car because you're an expert on cars and appreciate the engineering, or because it has comfortable seats, or because it's eco-friendly, or just because you like the colour.

7. It doesn't matter to readers how much effort went into your book. There's a scene in William Goldman's *Magic* (still one of the best unreliable-narrator thrillers ever written), in which the hero, Corky, an apprentice stage magician who has spent years practising card tricks for his big debut, finally cracks in the middle of the show and turns on the unresponsive audience, shouting: '*Do you know how hard that trick was? Do you know how many thousands of hours it took for me to master that lift?*'

Finally, when he has been escorted, still ranting, offstage, Corky realizes the truth: the audience doesn't know, or care.

Knowing and caring isn't their job. To make them pay attention – that's *yours*.

8. It's often at this point that some writers may feel the urge to blame the public. Don't. An author who sneers at their public has lost sight of what they are writing for.

9. So keep track of the bestseller lists. Instead of feeling envious or judgemental, try to identify *what it was* that made people want to buy those books. Was it a startling new idea? A comforting piece of escapism? It may be an ingredient you can include in your own writing. Assuming, that is, you want to.

10. Because, of course, not everyone wants to write something with a wide commercial appeal. Some actively seek to write commercially; others become bestsellers by accident. And some are aware from the start that they are writing something niche. There's nothing wrong with that at all. The book world is filled with different needs, and where would we be if *everyone* tried to write the same kind of thing?

10

Will a Creative Writing Course Help Me Succeed?

Writing courses come in many kinds. Some people find them helpful, some manage just fine without ever setting foot in a classroom. And writing courses – even university MA courses – are far from equal in terms of usefulness and quality. But there's no denying that they're big business. So, *should* you splash out on a writing course? And if so, how do you choose the right one?

1. You don't need to go on a course to become a writer. But a good writing course may, in some cases, give you the tools to become a better writer.

2. A good creative writing course doesn't need to be long, or expensive. A week-long Arvon Foundation course, a well-produced podcast – even a book – can deliver the same basic information as a year-long university course.

3. The social side can be one of the most useful aspects of following a writing course, giving you the opportunity to meet and share ideas with like-minded people.

4. **It can also be a means of giving yourself time and permission to write**, and to take your writing seriously.

5. **But the qualification in itself will not make any difference to whether or not your submissions are accepted by agents or publishers**, nor does it make publication any more likely. Any course that promises these things is suspect.

6. **Beware any writing course that spends too much time on things other than writing.** That means the process of submission, or writing pitches, or marketing your work, or explaining what agents do, etc. You can learn all this basic stuff online, and for free. When you're paying for an expensive course, stuff like this is just padding.

7. **There isn't a standard curriculum for creative writing courses.** There's no external body to check the standard of teaching, or the quality of the content of each course. It's up to you to choose wisely. Not all of them are worth the money.

8. **It's always worth checking who is tutoring the course.** Are they published authors? What do you think of their writing style? How successful are they? You don't have to be published to teach, of course, but beware an unpublished author claiming expertise on publishing.

9. **If your aim is to be published, find out who has previously been on the course.** Have any of them been published? If so, check them out. If no one has, you might want to rethink your choice.

10. **Not everyone wants to be published.** There are any number of other reasons to want to improve the quality of

your creative writing. Make sure that the course addresses this, and teaches you real and useful skills, rather than just giving you platitudes on how to write more commercially.

PART 9

Publication and Beyond

So now you're officially an author. Congratulations! After a long and challenging road, your book is finally in print. What happens now? Well, that depends on a number of things, and those things are changing all the time. This section deals with what professional writers *do*: and why getting published isn't the end of a journey, but only the first stage of something even more demanding . . .

Practise reading aloud.

1

It's Okay To Feel Good About This

Give yourself a round of applause. I mean it – do that right now. If you have a work in print, whether it's a self-published novel or a traditionally published novel, you *should* be feeling proud of yourself. Some people spend their whole lives talking about how they'd love to write a novel some day if only they could find the time, but you found the time, you stuck with it, you went through all the stages from first draft to publication. You endured rejections, disappointments, sacrifices, and you kept going. *You* did that. You deserve applause.

1. There's nothing wrong with celebrating your achievements. Too often authors are expected to play it cool, or to be 'modest' about their work. But here's the thing. In business – and you *are* in business now – people listen to what you say. And if you say you're second-rate, people will believe you.

2. That doesn't mean sounding off all the time about how wonderful you are. But it does mean banishing false modesty. If your local builder turned up to fix your leaky roof, and told you: *'I'm not really much of a builder, I don't* *know if you'll be satisfied*,' we both know he'd be out of the door like a shot.

3. If all this is very new to you, it's understandable to feel a little nervous. This is where the support of other authors can really help. Don't be afraid to seek advice, on social media or among the writing community. It's full of friends you haven't met, waiting to welcome you.

4. You may find that some of your writer friends withdraw from your circle. If that happens, it isn't your fault. But it's sometimes hard to come to terms with the success of a friend, when you're trying so hard to achieve that success for yourself. Leave them to work things out for a while. They'll either come around, or they won't.

5. It can be overwhelming to be published for the first time, and to suddenly have so many new things happening at once. If you can, try to put aside your fears and insecurities. Remind yourself that 99 per cent of writers may never reach this stage at all.

6. While you're enjoying the moment, don't forget to plan for the future. Be cautious with any money you've earned: now isn't the time to be looking at yachts.

7. It's never easy to think of your work as a commercial product to be sold. But if it's on sale, that's exactly what it is. This doesn't diminish your work, or you. Remind yourself of this from time to time.

8. Use what time you have to prepare. Things in publishing either move very slowly, or very fast.

9. Think about what you're going to need before you actually need it. Whether it's a working wardrobe, or some headshots, or some media training, or some public-speaking practice, or an accountant, you don't want to be doing any of this at the last minute.

10. Manage your expectations. You don't yet know where this journey will lead. But enjoy every step of the way, if you can – you're going on a hell of an adventure . . .

2

Know Your Rights

As a writer, published or unpublished, you own all the rights to your work – be they publishing rights, or media rights, or film rights (until you sell them, or otherwise sign them away). That means that no one is allowed to publish, or otherwise use or monetize your work, without your permission.

1. **Publishers – that's book publishers, or magazine publishers, or online publishers – need permission to publish your work.** Usually they pay you for this (and if they don't, you might need to think hard about what's in it for you).

2. **How much they pay you depends on just what they're publishing,** and also how well-known or successful you are, and how much the publishers think they're likely to make from publication.

3. **Some book publishers only buy publication rights in their own country,** but the larger ones will usually try to get universal rights – that is, book rights, film rights, media rights, and other publication rights – in all other countries around the world.

4. Some authors prefer to let their publishers handle these rights, rather than retain them for their agent to negotiate separately. This is fine, as long as the advance paid by the publisher reflects how much control over your work they've bought.

5. This is one of the reasons you might need an agent – or to ask the advice of the Society of Authors or the Authors' Guild – to check you're not signing away potentially lucrative rights to your publisher, to be sold on somewhere down the line with no financial benefit to you.

6. For instance, twenty years ago, lots of authors allowed their publishers to take e-book rights for peanuts, at a time when e-books weren't a thing. They are now, though, and those authors are losing out.

7. The same goes for film, audio, game development and other rights. If you give away or sell your rights, you don't own them any more, and unless there's a clause in the contract that says you get paid something afterwards, you don't earn anything more from them.

8. Also, some publishers are good at negotiating foreign or film rights, whereas some will acquire the rights, then just sit on them. This is a bit of a waste of your rights, which could be exploited to your benefit. A good agent will know how to do this.

9. So, guard your rights, people. Read the small print. Better still, get a real expert to read the small print.

10. And never, *ever* allow a publisher to give you a contract without a *reversion clause*. This gives you back your rights once a certain time has elapsed. Otherwise they'll own your rights for ever, and you'll never be able to move your list elsewhere.

3

Publicity

Publicity exists on any scale, from the self-promotion you might choose to do on your own social media to the kind of promotional tour organized by your publisher's publicity department. As a published author you would normally be expected to do a reasonable amount of promotion for your books, but given that no one really understands how much publicity that means, chances are you'll be pretty much able to decide for yourself what you're comfortable doing. Here are some things it might include:

1. **Book signings**. These are public signings, in which you typically sit in a bookshop for an hour, chatting and signing books for anyone who happens to turn up. Signed books sell better than unsigned ones; although this is a time-consuming thing to do, it can really help in the first week of publication (which is when sales really count).

2. **Readings**. Public readings, talks, etc., can be held in bookshops, libraries, church halls or at festivals. They typically take the form of a 20–30 minute talk, followed by a 10–20 minute reading, then Q&A with the audience. Books are usually on sale, so there's usually a signing afterwards. It's worth noting that audiences for events like these can

sometimes be very small – especially if you're a new author still looking to build a following. Don't be disheartened by this: it's not at all unusual at first to have an audience of ten people or fewer, but in these days of social media, all it takes is for one of them to be really impressed by your reading for word to get around very fast . . .

3. Festivals. There are lots of festivals, some more useful than others. Some offer a fee to speakers, some don't; but, as a rule, they're a good way to meet and connect with readers and other authors.

4. Book tours. Sometimes publishers will organize a promotional tour around the launch of a new book, usually lasting a couple of weeks, and consisting of multiple readings, interviews, festivals or book events. This gives the author the opportunity to raise awareness of their book, meet their readers and sign copies.

5. Stock signings. This is when an author goes into a series of bookshops – or sometimes the warehouse – just to sign stock. It isn't glamorous, but it does help sell books.

6. Foreign festivals. There are plenty of festivals abroad, too. Not all authors attend them, but if your book is popular, you may well be invited. Your publisher should always pay your travel, expenses and accommodation – after all, you're working on their behalf.

7. School visits. If you write for children or young adults, you may be asked to include school visits as part of your book promotion. If so, it can make a world of difference to make sure your visit is really well-planned by the school, with plenty of time for the pupils to prepare.

8. Conventions. Conventions differ from festivals in a number of ways – not least because, unlike literary festivals, attendees are usually expected to pay their own way (or have their publishers pay for them). Conventions are not primarily to sell books, but to interact with like-minded readers and writers within a specific genre (romance, or crime, or sci-fi and fantasy), and they can be a lot of fun, as well as giving you the chance to really participate in the genre community.

9. Digital media. This might include blog tours, online interviews, virtual festivals, blog posts. All this is great if you're the kind of person who feels uncomfortable speaking in public, and takes a lot less time than physically travelling.

10. Your publisher should also send ARCs (advance review copies) of your book to bloggers, influencers and reviewers. They may also send them to other authors in the hope of a jacket quote, a positive tweet or an Instagram post. It all helps spread the word on your book, and will contribute to the buzz.

4

Interviews

During the course of a book promotion, it's not unusual for you to be asked to give interviews – to journalists, radio presenters, bloggers, and anyone else with an interest in you and your book. Although interviewers are usually friendly, it's worth giving some thought to your approach.

1. There are a number of different kinds of interview, and it's worth approaching all of them with this in mind: *you* **are in charge**. It's not so much about what the interviewer wants you to say, but what *you* want them to come away with.

2. Press interviews. These can be face-to-face, or sometimes down a phone line. You'll probably find yourself answering the same kind of question lots of times, so make sure you've thought of what you really want to say.

3. If you don't feel comfortable answering a question, don't answer it. Some journalists specialize in making authors say things they didn't really want to say, or spinning what they actually said in a way that makes it more 'newsworthy'. Never feel pressured to give an answer to a question you find intrusive – just smile, move on and, if you can, change the subject to something you *do* want to discuss.

4. Email interviews. You may get these from bloggers, foreign journalists and anyone who isn't able to speak to you directly. It's useful at this stage to have an FAQ section on your website to give them some initial ideas, or you might find yourself writing the same basic answers over and over again.

5. Radio interviews. Sometimes these are down-the-line at a local radio station; others are conducted face-to-face in a studio. Many are live, or recorded as if they were live. Either way it's a good idea to approach *all* radio – like all TV – as if it's live.

6. Television interviews. Not all authors get interviewed on TV, but if you are, it's worth remembering that TV interviews tend to be very short, so it's useful to have a checklist of things you need to communicate. These might include the title of the book, a very short summary, why people should buy it and any future event you need to promote. By the time you've done all that, the interview may already be over.

7. It's also worth thinking about what you wear on TV. Stripes and close patterns tend to strobe on camera and if you're in a studio with a bright colour scheme, it might be a good idea to check it out first, and choose something that doesn't clash with the sofa.

8. Features. These tend to be longer and more in-depth, and will typically be for a magazine or a national newspaper. The interviewer may ask you general questions about yourself and your personal life as well as background about your book. Once again, it's up to you to deflect anything you're not comfortable talking about. Don't be afraid to do this: no one will hold it against you.

9. Just because an interviewer is warm and friendly to your face, it doesn't necessarily mean they'll be entirely positive about you in print. Don't tell them *anything* you're not comfortable making public. And don't assume that anything is going to be off the record. 'Author's Extraordinary Private Life' is a far more newsworthy story than 'Author Writes New Book'.

10. It's okay to turn down an interview. You don't have to talk to anyone you don't trust, or give interviews to a paper you don't like. You're not being paid to do this. There has to be something positive in it for you.

5

Festivals

Literary festivals are numerous, and they can be a lot of fun, both as a reader and as a writer. Here are a few things about them, to allow you to choose the ones that are right for you.

1. Literary festivals are often a terrific way to promote reading, books and literacy. They exist in all shapes and sizes all over the country, from the large, international ones – Hay, Edinburgh, Cheltenham – to smaller, local or more specialist events.

2. Publicists organizing author tours often use readings at festivals as the principal way of introducing a new book to the public. It can help new authors, too: readers may come to see an author they know, and stay to learn more about an author they've never read before.

3. It's a great way for authors to meet each other, too; and to feel connected to their readers. The online community can be great, but sometimes there's no substitute for a face-to-face meeting.

4. **Most festivals pay a small fee (on average, £200) to contributing authors**, as well as travel expenses and, if necessary, accommodation. Some, however, do not: it's worth finding out beforehand if a festival you're planning to support is equally willing to support *you*.

5. **Many festivals now send a contract to participating authors**: this ensures that both sides fulfil their obligations to the best of their ability. Read the contract carefully, or run it past your agent. Make sure it's fair, and that you're happy with all the details. (For example, is the festival planning to film your talk? Are they making extra money from this? Is there an exclusion clause that forbids you from doing a similar talk in the same area within a certain time scale? If so, does the fee you're receiving reflect this?)

6. **The best festivals pay fees to all contributors, large and small.** If you're being asked to pay your own expenses, or work 'for exposure', then consider offering your support to a festival that treats all contributors with equal respect.

7. **Apart from a fee and expenses,** a good festival should also provide you with general hospitality (drinks, sandwiches, etc.), a green room or similar in which to wait or prepare, an interviewer/presenter for your event and reasonable publicity surrounding your appearance.

8. **If you're unsure whether to try a new festival or not, look at the people they've invited in previous years.** If they have had a good and diverse range of guests, they're probably worth checking out.

9. Don't be afraid to ask other authors about their festival experiences. Too many authors are shy of asking what a colleague was paid, or whether they were treated well at a festival, or which ones they would recommend.

10. Conventions are not the same as festivals, although they can also be lots of fun. They're usually for genre writers – fantasy and sci-fi in particular do some excellent conventions, which can really help you get a feel for the community. They tend not to pay fees or expenses, though – so if you're attending as a speaker, you might want to ask your publisher if they're willing to contribute instead.

6

Prizes

Not every author wins prizes. Some bestselling authors go a whole lifetime without ever winning one; and some win prestigious prizes and never make it into the bestseller lists. But prizes are often great for introducing the public to authors and books they may not otherwise have known, and sometimes they offer a much-needed financial boost to struggling authors.

1. Literary prizes vary enormously in size and importance. Some are based on the popularity of the entrants, or on the sales of their latest book, or on the genre of the writing. But most of the highest-profile ones are for literary fiction.

2. Even if the entry requirements do not specify 'literary fiction', it often happens that genre books are winnowed out at an early stage 'because there are already prizes for crime, fantasy, etc.'

3. Many literary prizes only accept entries via publishers, although some allow self-published books, or even unpublished manuscripts. It's worth doing some research of your own on this – the Society of Authors, for instance, gives out £85,000 in prizes every year, in a variety of different areas, including children's fiction, translations, short stories, first novels, poetry and drama.

4. There's an important difference between a literary prize and a *writing competition*. Usually, writing competitions are not open to published writers, but serve as a means of discovering new talent. However, some writing competitions (and some that claim the more impressive title of 'literary prize') are downright useless in professional terms, and may even be exploitative and harmful to the entrants.

5. If you enter a writing competition, or submit your book for a prize, always look carefully at the terms of entry. How much are they charging you to enter? It's not unreasonable for a competition or prize to charge an entry fee (especially if they're paying their administrators), but some are just out to make money from the gullible.

6. Don't neglect the small print. What happens to your entry? Do the organizers get to keep the rights to your work? If so, beware. You'd be signing your work away – in some cases, even if you *didn't* win. Is it worth it?

7. Have a look at what's on offer. Is the prize itself worth winning? Sometimes, the prize is a sum of money. If so, great. Money always helps. If not, have a good look at what's on offer, and decide what would be in it for you.

8. Sometimes, the prize is a certificate, or a trophy, or basically 'exposure'. Ask yourself: *Have I heard of this prize? Have I heard of any of the winners?* If the answer's 'no', then clearly, the promise of exposure is meaningless.

9. Often, the prize is the promise of publication. This is a big, bright, sparkly lure, guaranteed to pulls in lots of entrants. However, if it's just publication in a self-published anthology that no bookshop will stock, it's also pretty much worthless.

10. Sometimes the prize is an Actual Book Deal with an Actual Publisher. If it is, you need to be even more careful. Have a good look at what the contract entails. Some of them can be incredibly exploitative. And, no – an exploitative book deal *isn't* better than no book deal at all. If your book is worth exploiting, then it's worth selling properly. A bad start could kill your career before it's even begun. If in any doubt at all, get in touch with the Society of Authors and ask their advice on whether a book deal is worth taking, or whether a writing competition is worth entering.

7

Reading

Reading your own work aloud may not always come easily. And yet, as an author, you're likely to be doing a lot of it, so you might as well get as good at it as you can. Here are a few things to think about when you're reading your work to an audience.

1. **If you're reading in public, don't spend all the time looking down at your book.** Look up from time to time. Pause. Make eye contact with the audience. Smile.

2. **Most people read faster when they're nervous.** Slow down. If you feel you're reading a bit too slowly, you're probably at just the right pace.

3. **Practise your microphone technique.** You'll need to speak more slowly into a mike than you would if you weren't using one. And watch out for plosive sounds, which can make the mike pop.

4. **Detach your sentences to avoid sounding fuzzy.** Remember that the sound of your voice takes longer to reach the back of a big room than a smaller space.

5. Audiences can be shy, too. If you're reading something funny, give the audience permission to laugh by looking up, making eye contact and smiling.

6. Don't feel the need to over-act or do exaggerated 'voices'. Just read with warmth and feeling.

7. Look as if you're enjoying yourself, and the audience will enjoy it, too. If you look embarrassed, bored or uncomfortable, you'll pass those feelings on to your audience.

8. Give a context to your reading by explaining to the audience where it comes in the book, and (briefly) what led up to it.

9. Don't go on for too long. Readings work best if you limit yourself to 10–15 minutes or so. Leave your audience wanting more.

10. Like any other skill, reading aloud takes practice. Record yourself reading aloud, and check out how you come across to an audience. Yes, you may feel awkward at first, but trust me, it will help.

8

Public Speaking

Public speaking doesn't come as naturally to some of us as to others. Nor is it always something a writer considers when they're sitting at their desk in their pyjamas, writing their first novel. But nowadays an author often needs to be a performer as well as just a writer, and so it's a good idea at this stage to practise your public speaking skills, and if you're a nervous public speaker, to learn to combat your stage fright. Here are a few ideas to try.

1. Most authors have stage fright at first. But if you are especially prone to nerves, try starting small. Get used to the sound of your own voice. Record yourself, and hear yourself back. Everyone hates hearing their own voice at first, but persevere, and it will help.

2. Prepare what you want to say. It's up to you how *much* you want to prepare: whether you want to script your whole talk word-for-word; or whether you can manage with bullet-point notes; or whether you'd rather not use notes at all.

3. Having no notes isn't as hard as it sounds, as long as you have a mental checklist of the things you want to say. It makes it easier to connect with your audience, and when you've done the talk a few times, you'll find it easier to duplicate. But if notes or a written script help you, go ahead, as long as you don't use them as an excuse not to look at your audience.

4. Practise your talk in front of someone you trust: your partner, your friend, your cat. What you're doing here is building mental muscle memory, so that when you're in front of a larger audience, you'll remember you've done this before.

5. If the visualizations in Part 1 helped you, you may want to try this one. Imagine yourself on stage in front of your friends and family. Visualize yourself speaking fluently and with enthusiasm. Imagine them laughing at your jokes, clapping and encouraging you. Know that they are all rooting for you. Visualize them there in the room when it comes to meeting your audience. Remind yourself that your audience will all be people like this. They came because they like your work. They are on your side.

6. People often advise you to imagine your audience on the toilet. Don't do that: it's creepy. Instead, imagine them hugging their kids, playing with their cat, making a batch of cookies, crying at a sad movie. You're here to make a human connection, not look down on them or feel superior.

7. Use a physical touchstone: a ring, or a meaningful object, small enough to carry with you. Say to yourself: *When I wear/carry this, I feel calm, charismatic and confident.* Do this every time you practise, and when you speak in public.

8. Or if you're more sensitive to sounds, choose a confidence-boosting song or a piece of music to get yourself

into the mood. Make it your anthem, your signature tune. Whatever you choose should be upbeat; play it just before an event, or imagine it playing on the PA as you go on stage.

9. Check out the room before you perform. Make sure the organizer of the event gives you a chance to see the place you're going to be using. Check the sound, the lectern or chair, get the feel of the microphone. The fewer unfamiliar things you have to cope with, the better.

10. It can be very helpful to share the stage with someone else. If the thought of performing solo still gives you the jitters, then maybe an in-conversation event would be easier to handle. Either find your own interviewer (preferably someone who knows you and your work, and can help give a natural direction to the conversation), or ask the event organizer to arrange an interviewer for you. Make sure you chat with them before your event. It makes a world of difference.

9

Going on Tour

Not all authors go on tour. This can be by choice, or because their publisher doesn't have the budget to pay for an extended tour. However, a well-organized tour of bookshops, libraries, schools and festivals is a good way of generating a buzz around a new book, and getting to meet your audience.

1. Tours are organized by your publicist, if you have one, and typically last about 2–3 weeks around publication. But you can organize your own if you have the time and resources.

2. You're not paid for touring (although many festivals now pay a token fee), but in any case, the publisher should pick up all your travel and accommodation expenses.

3. You'll typically do public readings and signings at various bookshops, festivals and libraries around the country, and maybe some interviews for radio and the press. You might also do digital or blog tours (which cost only time and effort), where you might do interviews or guest posts for a number of online publications.

4. If your book is published abroad, you might also do a foreign tour. This is usually at a different time to your UK tour, as it takes some months (or sometimes, years) for translations to come out. Even US editions often come out at a different time to the UK edition.

5. Touring can be interesting and fun, but it's also exhausting, hard work. It's not like going on holiday. Don't underestimate the amount of energy it takes to be talking about yourself, all day, every day, to groups of strangers, for a fortnight.

6. The best thing about book tours is often meeting your readers, and to have the chance to thank the publishers, booksellers, etc. who helped you. Books are about making human connections – here's your chance to do just that.

7. Pack light, sleep early and never, ever skip meals. You're going to need plenty of energy. And know your limits: if you find that you get exhausted after a week, make sure you (or your publicist) factor in more rest time.

8. Ask to see a draft schedule for every day/stage of your book tour. Make it clear to your publicist that nothing is confirmed until *you*'ve agreed it. That way you'll keep control of what you do, and how you'll approach it.

9. Meeting new people can be fun, but don't underestimate the drain on your energy. Make sure you get as much time alone as possible – either in your hotel room, or during the day, before events. Pace yourself, and don't overdo it: you don't want to be a wreck at the end of your tour.

10. It's important to know when to distance yourself. Yes, you want to connect with your readers. You may even make friends with some of them. But do beware meeting your readers outside the context of a festival or literary event. That's not being suspicious or aloof; its common sense and self-care. It's better to take sensible precautions at first than to have to deal with a stalker later on.

10

Requests and Demands

Even full-time authors find themselves struggling to manage their time. The more success you have, the more you'll find other people wanting to claim your time. They may ask you for other things, too: some are okay, others are not. Here are some of the most common demands and requests for you to look out for.

1. Endorsements. That usually means a quote that can be printed on the cover of a new release. Except in the case of personal friends, most authors prefer these requests to come via their agents or publishers, rather than directly or through social media. It's up to you to decide whether or not you want to give someone a quote: authors tend to get a *lot* of these requests, so don't feel obliged to respond unless you really want to.

2. To 'just look over' a manuscript. Unless the author is a close personal friend (and even in most cases, if they are), please don't do this. Manuscript evaluation is a specialist skill, and to ask an author to do a week's work for free is completely unacceptable. And if you *do* accept to read an unpublished manuscript from a stranger, be warned: you may be letting yourself in for months – even years – of harassment. You may even be accused of having stolen their idea. For your own protection, it's best to just say no.

3. Free books. Lots of people assume that an author has unlimited copies of their book to give away. We don't. We get a small number of complimentary copies of our books from the publishers (usually about a dozen), but once they're gone, we have to buy them from shops, just like anyone else. So unless you want to give a signed copy away to a charity, or as part of a giveaway, it's fine to ignore most of these requests.

4. To 'just pass on' a manuscript (or CD, or film script) to someone you know (your editor, your agent, J.K. Rowling). You can safely decline any requests like this one. Authors are not postal workers. They're not there to deliver messages to friends and colleagues in the business.

5. To 'help someone get published'. We get a lot of requests like this, so you might want to draft a standard reply, letting the person down gently. Authors are not publishers, and whatever their profile, they can't help anyone get a book deal.

6. To work for 'exposure' (see also: 'We don't have a budget' and 'We can give you lunch'). Don't be taken in by this kind of approach. If the person values your work, they should expect to pay for it. Some authors may choose to support a non-profit organization or a charity, but that's their choice. It should never be assumed that an author is prepared to work for free.

7. Marketing slogans (see also: 'Just a few words'), in exchange for a free sample of the merchandise. Again, don't be taken in by this. Someone is asking you to do a market-eer's job without offering a marketeer's fee.

8. Selfies, signatures, etc. Authors are usually happy to give these at events, although if someone asks you for a selfie or an autograph when you're off-duty in a restaurant, or with your family, or in the shower at the gym, don't feel you have to oblige them. They're crossing a line.

9. To write an article for free. Many online publications (and some print ones) don't pay their journalists. Even so, they can often find someone to contribute a piece. You may find that in the case of an organization with a wide reach (e.g. the *Huffington Post*) it helps your profile to contribute. On the other hand, consider that every time an author works for free, it makes it harder for the rest to ask to be paid. And in a world in which *everyone* consumes the work of creators and storytellers, we need to encourage people to value that work, and to pay creators fairly.

10. Time. Authors are constantly fielding other people's demands on their time. Even full-time authors find it a challenge to give enough time to their writing. Some things come with the territory (book events, promotion); other projects are up to you. But there will come a point at which you need to say no, even to things that sound really great: that Australian book tour, that project you would love to do if you had a free six months. **Learn to say no. It's a vital skill.** Your main work has to take precedence.

PART 10

Welcome to the Dark Side

This is what you dreamed of. You're finally doing what you wanted. So why doesn't it always feel the way you imagined it would? Why does your subconscious persist in giving you these feelings? Here are a few of the challenges authors sometimes encounter.

1. Dealing With Fear
2. Coping With Failure
3. Rejection
4. Writer's Block
5. Imposter Syndrome
6. Anxiety
7. Guilt
8. Second Novel Syndrome
9. When Your People Let You Down
10. When It Just Doesn't Happen

Chasing the Plot Bunny.

Locating the Troubleshooting Flamingo.

Shooing the Impostor Syndrome Butterfly.

Ignoring the Prevarication Tortoise.

Fleeing the Hippopotamus of Rejection

1

Dealing With Fear

To be a writer is to live with fear. Fear of rejection, of failure, of not meeting our own expectations. Nearly all of us live with this, but the worst of it is thinking that we are alone. We're not: and although just knowing that doesn't mean the fear goes away, I hope it can make it easier to bear.

1. First, know that feeling afraid is absolutely normal. Every writer you know feels afraid – and the feeling seldom goes away. Thus, every word you write is an act of courage. The objective is not to banish the fear, but to understand it for what it is.

2. Next, decide what the fear represents. Is it a fear of rejection? Well, rejection is always a possibility. But remember, every writer you admire has been rejected many times. If it happens, you'll be in good company. And you'll learn from the experience.

3. Are you afraid of being laughed at? No one who writes books, or who works in the book industry, will do that. They know how much courage it takes to put yourself out there. The writing community is very supportive. We all want you to succeed.

4. Are you afraid of not being good enough? Welcome to the club. Writers seldom ever feel entirely satisfied with their work. That's because we're all on the same learning curve. And the moment you feel you have nothing to learn, you've stopped growing.

5. Are you afraid of being judged? That's going to happen the moment you send your work out into the wild. Whoever you are, whatever your talent, there will be people who don't like your work. But there will also be people who do.

6. Are you afraid of being hurt? That too can happen. But writing is like love – you have to accept the possibility of being hurt in order to reap the benefits of being loved. You can't escape that, so embrace it. Be honest and true. That's all you can do.

7. Are you afraid of never being a 'proper writer'? Impostor syndrome is incredibly common among authors. Remember that behind the glossy photograph on the dust-jacket, there's someone who once was where you are now, and who may feel just as you do.

8. Are you afraid of the blank page? Then put some words down on it. They don't necessarily have to be good words. But keep writing, and the good words will come in their own time.

9. Are you afraid you'll let yourself down? Maybe stop setting yourself such high standards. Don't set goals you can't easily achieve. Be kinder to yourself. Approach your project line by line, minute by minute, and eventually, you'll get there.

10. Are you afraid that everyone else knows a secret short-cut that you don't know about? Don't be. There are no shortcuts. The journey may be a long one, but every word you write is a step forward. Even the ones you cut have already taught you something.

2

Coping With Failure

To many, '*Failure isn't an option*' is supposed to be an empowering mantra. In fact, it's a silly and dangerous piece of self-delusion. Here's why.

1. Everyone encounters failure on the road to success. The only way to avoid it is NEVER TO TRY AT ANYTHING.

2. To fail is not a bad thing. It is a wholly necessary thing. You have to fall over many times before you learn to walk.

3. Having failed at something does not make YOU a 'failure'. It means you tried at something. If you try it again, you have a better chance of success because of it.

4. Early success often leads to complacency, rather than competence. High achievers at school often end up getting lazy and giving up at the first sign of trouble.

5. Failure is opportunity. Sometimes, a failure in one thing can lead to an unexpected success in another field.

6. Every successful person you have ever heard of has failed at some stage in their career. They kept going. So can you. That's why you've heard of them.

7. **As long as you are pushing yourself, failure will always be an option.** Learn to use it and learn from it, rather than to erase it.

8. **Failure makes you stronger.** Every time you fail, you come back with new resources, new experience and new determination.

9. **Failure is a teacher. Each misstep is a lesson.** Make sure you are open to the lessons experience offers you. Don't fall into despondency, or wrongly blame other people.

10. **Not succeeding is not quite the same as failing.** The only real failure is, either through fear or laziness, not to make the attempt at all.

3

Rejection

However good you are, however experienced you are, however lucky you are, the minute you decide to approach someone else with your work, you're going to get rejections. Accept it. It comes with the territory. And, however successful a writer becomes, it's always a possibility.

1. Rejection never gets any easier, but there are ways to deal with it. Remember that a rejection of your project is not a rejection of *you*: it just means that your book wasn't right for the person you sent it to.

2. Some rejections are actually useful: they can provide you with clues as to why your book was rejected, and, where appropriate, how to fix what's wrong. Always thank anyone who gives you feedback: it means they think you're worth their time.

3. Some rejections are generic, providing you with nothing but a standard 'Not for us, thanks.' Either way, don't argue – not even if you're 100 per cent sure they didn't read your submission. They didn't have to.

4. Don't hit back at the person rejecting you, or rant or complain about them online. Rejection is a rite of passage, an endurance test that you need to pass before you can face the next – and considerably harder – stage.

5. Avoid unnecessary rejection by making sure you submit your work in the right way, and to the right people. Take time to research the submission guidelines of agents and publishers, and follow them.

6. Work on something new while you wait for a response to your submissions. Taking time away from your project will give you the objectivity to deal with any potential changes you may need to make, and it means that if your book is accepted, you'll already be halfway through a new one.

7. Lots of great books get rejected at first. That doesn't necessarily mean your book is one of them. Be persistent, but be humble enough to take criticism, too.

8. Give yourself some time to gain a little objectivity, then look carefully at your manuscript again. Decide what needs to be done to make it more acceptable. If necessary, bring in an independent manuscript evaluator or editor to help you knock it into shape.

9. Know when to put a project aside. If you can't get it to work, make something else. And don't obsess over the time you spent on an abandoned project – NOTHING you write is ever wasted. It's all part of the learning process.

10. Don't blame the publishing business for not seeing your potential. Although there are examples of great books that never make it, if yours is rejected repeatedly and universally, there's probably a reason for that. Keep writing, keep submitting, and learn from your rejections.

4

Writer's Block

A great deal of misinformation surrounds the concept of writer's block. In fact, it's a possible symptom of underlying mental illness, and it's less common than most people think. However, many writers use the term loosely, to mean 'lacking the will or the inspiration to write'. If this is you, try to identify the reason.

1. Do you have anxiety? Don't try to force yourself to write. Anxiety is often at the root of writer's block and associated problems, and putting yourself under pressure just feeds it. If you think you need therapy for your anxiety, get it. Your work will wait until you're ready.

2. Have you fallen out of love with your work-in-progress? It happens to the best of us. Try writing something else for a while – fan fiction, blog posts, a short story. Give yourself a break for a bit, and start seeing other projects. You'll return to your work-in-progress with renewed enthusiasm.

3. Have you been discouraged by rejection or criticism? You're not alone. Seek out other writers, share your thoughts. Try to find out why it happened. Learn what you can from the experience. Remember that rejection is an unpleasant, but unavoidable, part of being a writer.

4. Are you afraid of being judged? It's hard to send a project out. Many people would rather *be writing* a book than to *have written* one. Having written a book means making yourself vulnerable to the opinions of readers. It takes courage. But unless you do, you can't move on to the next level.

5. Are you tired and overworked? Give yourself a break. Writers can sometimes make unrealistic demands of themselves. Stop testing yourself to destruction. Ideally, go on holiday, but if that's not an option, just put your laptop aside for a week. Do other things. Take the pressure off. You may find it helps you focus when you return.

6. Are you short of ideas? Maybe you're not reading enough. Go back to reading for pleasure, and be sure to read as widely as you can. You can't produce art unless you also consume it at an equal rate. If you find the books you're reading too taxing or work-related, go back to reading what you love. Remember how much you enjoy it.

7. Are you short of time? Go back to a basic writing routine. Start by writing only 300 words a day, every day. It will get you back into a manageable routine without taking up too much of your busy schedule.

8. Look at your surroundings. Is your workspace right for you? I use a SAD lamp in winter because otherwise I don't seem to be able to concentrate. If you're sensitive to seasonal changes, maybe look into motivational lighting options for your workspace. If you can, go out. Get some air. Do something physical. Your body and your brain will thank you for it. If your workspace is feeling stale, change things round. Find somewhere new to work. Change the font on your work-in-progress. Try writing longhand for a while. It may help you out of your rut.

9. Are you spending too much time alone? Being with other people often helps banish the doldrums. Don't shut yourself away. See your friends. Socialize. Go out. Listen to people on public transport. Human stimulus is often at the heart of creativity.

10. Are you on a deadline? If you are, you may be feeling under too much pressure. Tell whoever is waiting (publisher, agent, etc.) as soon as you can if you think you won't meet your deadline. They'll understand. It will help their planning, and take unwelcome pressure off you.

5

Imposter Syndrome

(People struggling with imposter syndrome often worry about whether it's actually spelt 'impostor syndrome'. Don't worry, it's all good.)

1. Imposter syndrome affects a large number of creators, artists, writers and performers. If you have it, you're in excellent company.

2. One of the most common symptoms is the feeling that you're not a 'proper' writer, and that you don't fit in to the writing community. Given how many writers feel this way, I would be more surprised if you *didn't*.

3. Imposter syndrome doesn't go away just because someone gets to be famous or successful. In fact, it often gets worse. That's because it's an irrational belief, which has nothing to do with your fame or success.

4. It isn't just about 'feeling shy' or 'being a bit awkward'. It can be crippling. Don't minimize your problem. Get help, and seek the support of others.

5. **There's no single, easy way to deal with it.** But it does help to remember how common it is. You are not alone.

6. **Although men do get imposter syndrome, women are more likely to feel it.** This may be partly to do with the historical (though sadly still current) view that art created by women matters only to women, whereas art created by men is universal. Either way, take it seriously, and make sure other people do, too. You don't need to suffer in silence.

7. **It helps to talk to other people in your situation.** This is much easier nowadays. Social media allows us to share our experiences – and our insecurities – as creators.

8. **Authors, it might help to join the Society of Authors.** I've met so many authors who were eligible to join but didn't think of themselves as 'proper' authors. Membership of a professional association might give you the confidence boost you need.

9. **Try to identify the things that bring out your imposter syndrome** (with me it's usually parties), and the things that can help reduce it. Try not to go to an event alone. Don't compare yourself with other people.

10. **Remember that it's also okay not to do an event that makes you feel uncomfortable.** It's not the end of the world if you miss a party. But before you creep out of a crowded room early, check that there isn't someone standing there looking as awkward as you feel. You might just make a friend …

6

Anxiety

If you're an author, chances are you've had anxiety symptoms at some time or another. Whether these are mild or
severe, it's worth acknowledging and dealing with, because
so many non-writers assume that a writer's life is easy and
privileged, and that therefore those with mental-health issues
are just being writerly and over-dramatic.

1. If this is you, the first thing to do is to **acknowledge your
feelings.** They are valid and justified; and you share them
with the majority of writers, whether they are struggling to
be published or whether they are already successful.

2. Get help if you need it. There's no shame in seeking
medical help to solve the problems that are impacting on
your life and your writing. If your anxiety has a particular focus, try to identify what can be done to address the
cause.

3. Are you financially insecure? Lots of authors are. Having
a second job is one way of feeling less stressed financially, and
remember – you are no less of a writer if you only write at
weekends than if you write full time.

4. Are you getting enough emotional support? Families and friends, however loving, can sometimes not quite understand what it's like. Seek out like-minded people. The Society of Authors is a good place to start: it can give writers the chance to meet, and to discuss the issues that concern them.

5. Are you pushing yourself too hard? If you're holding down a day job, participating in family life *and* writing furiously in your spare time, consider slowing down a bit. There's no rule that says you have to be unhappy to make good art. Take time to smell the roses.

6. Success has its own unique stresses, which can often be compounded by feelings of guilt that you're not happier and more grateful for your success. That's your anxiety speaking, right there, telling you that you don't deserve nice things. You do.

7. Are you putting your writing and promotion duties ahead of your physical and mental needs? Are you missing out on meals, sleep, exercise, or seeing your friends? Prioritize your well-being. Make sure the people you work with do, too.

8. Lots of full-time writers suffer from a lack of daily routine, especially when they're travelling, or have lots of public events to do. Try to find ways of keeping some kind of a routine, even if it's only going for a walk at the same time every morning.

9. Public events can be stressful, even if you enjoy them. It's easy to get overwhelmed and hyped-up, which in turn makes it hard to sleep, and leads to exhaustion. Don't underestimate the time you need to be alone and to recover.

10. Don't put yourself under too much pressure, or allow anyone else to do so. Tell your publishers loud and clear when you need to be left alone, or if a deadline is stressing you. And most importantly, learn to say no. FOMO is a killer.

7

Guilt

We've all been there. Writer's guilt. It's the reason so many of us put ourselves down, tell people we're not 'proper' writers, agree to work for free and say things like, 'It's not as hard as working down a mine.' It's also bullshit. Here's why.

1. Writers feel more than our fair share of guilt. That's because we've been fed the myth of the 'purity' of art, and the artist as the 'chosen one'. In fact, art comes from hard work, luck, some ability, and a lot of persistence.

2. The ability to write well is no different to any other acquired skill. Learning Russian, being a chef, being a plumber, training as a gynaecologist. And yet, no one with these skills feels the need to apologize for them. Why should you?

3. Whether you're a professional writer or an enthusiastic amateur – and especially if you're a woman – you've probably been made to feel guilty at one time or another for giving your writing priority over family life or other responsibilities. And yet, it's likely that the same people wouldn't dream of making you feel guilty over going to the gym, or going shopping, or going out for drinks with a friend. Your free time is your own, not theirs.

4. Remind yourself that whether writing is your job or your hobby, you're allowed to give it the time it needs. You're not being selfish, any more than your friends are being selfish for doing their jobs, or enjoying their hobbies.

5. Remember that you're allowed to feel proud of your achievements and successes. You worked hard. You earned them.

6. You're also allowed to keep enjoying what you do, regardless of publication or commercial success. And whatever your ambitions, you're allowed to take your writing as seriously as you want to.

7. If you ever doubt this, think of all the people who enjoy sport, even though they have no desire to be professional runners, squash players, or footballers. They enjoy what they do. It's good for them. They feel proud when they win. So should you.

8. Fiction is one of the UK's biggest exports, generating billions every year. And yet, very little of this goes to the creators. That's often because their writer's guilt is being exploited by those with an interest in making them feel worthless.

9. Some writers attribute their success to luck. And, yes, luck does have a part to play. But not without hard work, persistence and skill. Luck is winning the lottery. All tickets have an equal chance. But art isn't like that.

10. And lastly, don't feel guilty if you have 'nothing to show' from your writing. If it brings you joy, a sense of achievement, a connection with others, a heightened sense of empathy, or just a warm feeling inside, then it has already shown you plenty.

8

Second Novel Syndrome

You may well have already heard the phrase 'that diffi-cult second novel', and wondered why it's so common. Having written and published one novel, surely it gets easier? Well, yes and no. Certainly, the techniques you learn while writing your first book will serve you well for the second. But a second novel can feel very different to writing a first – especially if the first one has had any kind of success. Here's why.

1. You have unlimited time to write a first novel, but only a year to write a second. If your first novel has had any success at all, publishers and readers will be eager to see another as soon as possible. That's why, when you're submitting work, you should already be thinking about the next project. It helps to have half a draft of something new under your belt in case your first project does take off.

2. Expectation is a curse. This applies especially when the first novel has been a big success: basically, the greater the success, the greater the pressure on the author to follow it up with something equally popular.

3. Most second novels don't get the same coverage as a debut. The industry is obsessed by debuts, which means that you're likely to get more of your publisher's attention for your first novel than for your second.

4. In some cases, the author is pressured to rush out a second novel to capitalize on the success of a previous bestseller. This can mean that essential editing and rewriting isn't done, and the book suffers as a result.

5. In traditional publishing, it's often a case of, 'Two strikes and you're out.' That means that if your first novel *hasn't* been a big success, the second novel is often seen as an author's last chance to break through.

6. That means that the sales of your second novel may determine whether a publisher keeps you on. If a book does well, they're more likely to renew an author's contract. If it doesn't, they may not.

7. Publishers will often use the first novel's sales figures to project sales of the second. If the first did very well, they will assume the second will be a bestseller, too. This is not always the case, however.

8. This isn't necessarily because the second book isn't as good. But first novels generally get more attention, more prizes, kinder reviews and more sympathetic press coverage. With second novels, the knives come out.

9. Some authors whose first novels become bestsellers assume that their second novel will be equally well received. It can be bitterly disappointing when the second gets less attention, fewer sales (and therefore far smaller subsequent advances).

10. That's why it's worth taking time to make sure your second novel is completely right before publishing – in spite of any pressure from your publisher. A good first novel can make your name, but a really good second one can ensure the continuation of your writing career.

9

When Your People Let You Down

Relationships are important in this job. Most writers rely heavily on their agents, their editors, their publishers. Many come to regard them as friends. An author's relationship with their agent is a kind of marriage, which, if it fails, can feel as traumatic as a divorce. The same is often true with editors and publishers. We trust them. We have to. And yet – they sometimes let us down, and we have to deal with that, too.

1. Always remember that, however much you may like your agent (or your editor, or your publisher), they are doing a job, and that however much they may like *you*, they're in this for the money.

2. It never gets any easier if your publisher lets you go, or your agent decides they can't represent you any more. Remind yourself it isn't about *you*. This is business, and you mustn't take it personally. Don't say anything you will regret. Things may change in the future: you may even find yourself working together again some day.

3. Sometimes, an agent may turn out to be less than trustworthy. Fortunately this doesn't happen often, but you can – and should – help protect yourself.

4. First, make sure you go with an agent who is a member of the Association of Authors' Agents or similar, and has agreed to their code of practice. That gives you somewhere to go if you have a problem with your agent.

5. Second, make sure you have a written contract with your agent. It doesn't have to be much: just a record of your agreement, and the amount of notice each of you needs to give (usually 1 to 3 months) before terminating the relationship.

6. Third, go over your contracts carefully or, preferably, have them read by an expert. The Society of Authors has a free contract service which will look over your contracts for you, and flag up anything they think is questionable. Agents are busy people, often with many other clients, and have sometimes been known to overlook a small, but important detail. Basically, **trust your agent, but have your contracts checked anyway.**

7. Same goes for your publisher. Trust your people to be human, to be fallible and to put their own business interests first, and you'll never be disappointed.

8. If an editor lets you down, it's most likely to be about their approach to your work. Are they trying to take creative control? Have they forgotten that they're your editor, and not the co-author of the book? Or is it the other extreme – you feel they're just not contributing enough to the process? Either way, it's important to get the relationship right. Talk to them directly. Tell them your concerns. And if that doesn't work, request another editor.

9. Or you could hire your own independent editor. In-house editors, like in-house publicists, can sometimes be over-burdened, and an independent editor might be more likely to give their full attention to your work.

10. Whatever happens, don't allow a disappointing professional relationship to sour your pleasure in your writing. Remember why you came into this in the first place. Keep the joy in your work alive. *That's* the relationship that really counts.

10

When It Just Doesn't Happen

We all know what this is like. You put all your energy into a project, you spend years planning and preparing for it, sometimes it even gets almost all the way to completion, you get your hopes up, you can almost taste success – and then, one day, suddenly, *pffft!* It disappears. The company goes under, the investors pull out, a recession hits, a key person loses interest. Suddenly, the project to which you've given years of your life – a book, a film deal, a play, a TV show – just isn't happening any more. It feels like a bereavement. And the worst thing is, unlike a bereavement, the people around you don't always understand how deep your sense of loss may go. After all, you can always find another project. Can't you?

1. The more successful and experienced you get, the more likely this is to happen at some point or another. Trust me, it never gets any easier. But knowing you're not alone can help.

2. Give yourself permission to grieve. You're entitled to your feelings. They are completely understandable.

3. It's not always about the money. Even if you were paid a fee for writing a TV series that never gets made, it's natural to feel as if you've lost a part of yourself. Don't let anyone tell you that your sense of loss isn't real.

4. Don't feel the need to move on straightaway. Disappointment like this often results in a loss of interest in writing, or a sense of discouragement that won't go away. This is natural. Don't fight it. Don't put yourself under any further pressure.

5. Give yourself a break. Take a holiday, if you can. Go back to doing things for yourself: reading old favourites, watching favourite films, walking in the countryside. Do the things you would do for yourself if you were in recovery after a long and painful illness: you are convalescing. Recovery takes time.

6. It's okay *not* to get back on the horse. If you really don't want to take on a similar project again, don't feel you have to. It's your choice, no one else's.

7. Don't throw valuable time at a dead project. Yes, giving up can be painful. But sometimes you have to plough over your crop in order to plant something else.

8. It's fine to cannibalize or reuse anything you can salvage. Maybe your project didn't work as a TV show, but perhaps it could become a part of something else. Still attached to those characters? Put them into something else. Think that plot line could work elsewhere? Maybe it could be a book or a game, a radio play, a short story.

9. One day you may feel like trying again. When that happens, give it your all. Creativity is like the leaves on a tree; the fact that they fall in autumn doesn't mean new shoots won't come back.

10. Remind yourself once again that *nothing you create is ever wasted*. Anything can be rebuilt. Even a shattered project can be reused for parts. Right now, you can't know how this might feed into future projects; but hold fast, keep going, and maybe it will.

Afterword

And yes, you *will* keep going, right? After all, you've got this far. You may not have achieved everything you wanted – yet. But whenever it feels as if you're writing in a vacuum, remember that what you do matters. Every act of creation brings hope. Every little thing you build lifts you a little higher. And even if all you ever gain is the feeling of having made something good, pleasure is an end in itself. Joy is never wasted.

But *giving* joy – that's something else. There's nothing like having an audience. Writing fiction is all about making connections. A story – the *right* kind of story – can reach across continents. A story can change the course of a life. The right words, in the right order, can accomplish anything. Why do we write? To communicate. To make that human connection. To share something joyous and intimate, and to know that you are not alone.

Ray Bradbury said it this way. *'Fall in love and stay in love. Write only what you love, and love what you write. The word is love. You have to get up in the morning and write something you love, something to live for.'*

That's why you need to keep going. The world needs your stories as much as it ever did. And when I say *your* stories, I mean *all* the stories that haven't been told, all the voices that haven't been heard: older voices, younger voices, neurodiverse voices, BAME voices, LGBTQ voices, voices from people with different backgrounds and experiences.

Diverse voices are still all too rare in mainstream publishing. And yet, publishers – and readers – need them more than ever. And one of the reasons there are so few alternatives to the mainstream narrative is that sometimes, people hesitate to put their voices out there. I hear too many new writers asking: *Am I a proper writer yet?* And I get it: it took me close to twenty years to accept that, however different I might *feel* from so many other writers – London literary novelists; writers from more privileged backgrounds; people brought up to believe that not only did they have *permission* to write, but that it was *expected* of them – I was allowed call myself a writer without feeling that somehow I'd managed to gate-crash a very exclusive party. Some literary novelists can sometimes make you feel that way. But if you write, you're a writer. And if you're a writer, you deserve the chance to follow your story as far as it will lead you.

Remember, too, that just writing is an act of bravery. You have the courage to do what it takes to give your voice the chance to be heard. Don't do it because you want to be the next J.K. Rowling, or Maya Angelou, or Margaret Atwood. Those are already taken. Do it because your voice is unique. Only you can take this chance. No one else will ever be you, or tell your story the way you can.

So writers, write: with joy and love. You may not all take your stories as far as you'd like to take them. But write them, and send them into the world like dandelion seeds on the wind, because love and joy exist to be shared, and maybe, one day, they'll come back to you.

Acknowledgements

It takes a village to build a book. This one was brought to you by the hard work of many people: my agent, Jon Wood at RCW; the excellent folk at September Press; commissioning editor Hannah McDonald, managing editor Charlotte Cole, copyeditor Belinda Jones, proofreader Beth Hamer. Thanks also to Clare Skeats, for her cover design; Ed Pickford, for the typesetting; David Francis, for the ebook conversion; Sue Amaradivakara, for publicity; and Ian West and Claire Thompson in sales and marketing. Because of you, this book is better laid out, better designed, more accurate, and more likely to find its audience. And most of all, thanks to the loyal followers of my #TenTweets hashtag, without whom I would probably never have thought to write this book in the first place. There are far too many of you to name, but you know who you are, and I see you. Without readers, a writer is nothing but the sound of one hand clapping. But together, we can be heard. Let's get ready to make some noise . . .